I DON'T WANT TO TALK ABOUT IT

Raphael James

IN DEDICATION

to my father Leroy James and my mother his faithful
caregiver.
To my son Grant "The Champ" thank you for patiently
teaching me how to be a better father.
To his mother Sarena, you are both amazing and
beautiful. Our lives are better because of you.
To my girls, Jaydn and Nia, you are brilliant
lights. Thank you for the beautiful ways you have shown
up for your brother.

And to you the reader, the one who suffers in silence,
the one who tries to hold it together for everyone else,
the one who would just as soon leave the room before
anyone saw you break down and cry...this is for you.
Breathe. It's finally time to talk about it.

Contents

Prologue

For 31 years, I have made it my life's work to tell other people's stories. And yes, I get it if the title of this book may sound a bit hypocritical.

As a veteran television news reporter and anchor, my mission has always been to effectively convey accurate information, promptly, with tact and dignity. For hours on end, I've gone live from the scene of chemical leaks, hurricanes, hostage standoff situations, and even a church massacre. On far too many occasions, my face delivered the life-changing news that a community member or loved one would not be coming back home.

No joy is gleaned from being the bearer of bad news. Evil things happen in life and I don't have the power to stop them. However, I hope the weight of the words lands a little softer, coming from a trusted friend. I pray that the spaces between my words are filled with comfort, light, and empathy.

My calling as a journalist is to inform and make aware. Even when the message is hard to hear, I will deliver it to my audience. When they can't make the city council meeting because they're just leaving work, I've got them. When the language behind the school board tax increase is confusing, I'm there to help walk them through it and hold elected officials to account.

I have never run from difficult and/or unpleasant conversations. But when it comes to my own story...my father's diagnosis of dementia and his eventual death, and my only son's diagnosis of autism spectrum disorder and the hell that my family has endured, coupled with a high and holy God who allows any of it to happen in the first place, I DON'T WANT TO TALK ABOUT THAT!

But somebody's got to have the conversation. Someone has to address the "elephants in the room", so it might as well be me. Let's see where this goes.

Introduction

Outfitted in my all-black suit, I sat down before the mirror and watched my reflection judge me. I glanced down at my weapon and traced my finger along its barrel.

"This is it," I thought. "I'm not running away from this anymore."

My fingers slowly tightened their grip. I raised it...and squeezed.

Hot red rage spilled across the page. Curses stained the paper, baptized by my tears. And when the words stopped coming, when my chamber lay empty, I placed my weapon back on the table.

My weapon? A pen. Mightier than a sword, less messy than a gun, and not nearly as permanent. But this process has been painful...painfully necessary.

I hate doing this. But I won't be able to sleep until I let some of this ~~blood~~...ink run out of my ~~veins~~...~~fingers~~...pen.

If I were an artist I'd sketch a man hooked up to an IV drip. The crimson liquid is draining from his forearm and running along his finger bleeding out onto the white pages of his journal.

That's how it feels to do this.

I beg for peace, but my brain won't let me find it. Too many neglected thoughts now clamor for my attention.

They all want to tumble onto the pages, but I'm doing a decent job, of keeping them at bay, by writing about anything else I can think.

It's my way of creating a dam. A way of keeping my damn thoughts dammed up inside.

Why do you want to come out here, so badly? Is it that crowded in there? You should keep each other company and leave me alone.

Now I know why people do drugs and drink alcohol.

It's a way to drown you out. Keep you quiet so that I can get some peace. But I don't want to be drowned. I want you to leave me alone.

I know that all of you aren't bad. Most of you are good memories. But the good on the backdrop of what will never be again is a lot to handle.

Why should I allow my thoughts to take me where THEY want to go?

I WANT TO GO TO SLEEP! Meet me there in the form of a dream. Then we can both get what we want.

1

Please Don't Make Me Talk

July 27, 2020

Don't make me talk. I'm barely holding it together right now and if I start to talk about it I don't know what will happen. Please don't make me talk.

I'm a broken man right now. Shattered. But I am still the *form* of a man. I am precariously held together by strips of pride. It's not pretty. It doesn't feel good…but at least I recognize myself.

In my silence, I can be strong or at least appear so. I do not feel strong, but I am a man. It is so important to me that YOU believe that I am strong. THAT, is enough for me at this moment. If I can't actually command strength, please remember those times when I was strong.

Please don't make me give voice to my troubles. Please don't ask me to crumble in defeat in your arms. Please don't ask me to admit that I've done all I can do, and it's still not enough.

Please. For the love of God, if you love me don't make me confront God at this late hour. I don't want to be forced to acknowledge that I've been writing scripts for God to come in and be the hero in this story and that he's missed his cue EVERY. SINGLE. TIME.

If you love me, please let me manage my thoughts alone until morning. You know they say joy comes in the morning…

There I go again. Writing God into another winning scenario. Broken man that I am, I'm still a man. Let me drift off to sleep with that intact. I failed today. I'll try again tomorrow, probably.

It's not you. It's definitely me. It's not that I can't talk to you, I just don't want crumbs in my bed. If I start talking right now the best parts of me will begin to crumble. Those parts that I think you appreciate the most…the fearlessness, the confidence, the air of reassurance.

Please don't make me talk.

Please.

I love you.

2

Writing It Out

Sarena James, Photo Credit

I've told many people's stories, but the one person I rarely talk about is myself. I don't particularly get joy in talking about me and the way that I'm feeling. When people ask how I'm doing, "fine" or "great" is usually the standard answer. I don't bother going deeper than that, especially if they don't press.

I enjoy being able to help others, but I'm hardwired to want to help myself. If I could, I would go through life without having to rely on anyone else to get me what I needed. If God himself would fulfill any request I made of him, I would be happy...I think.

But it doesn't seem to work that way. When things have gotten particularly hard for me to handle, the only way through has been the intervention of others financially and emotionally. I believe in God; I believe he exists. But he makes me have to deal with other people far more regularly than I would like.

This topic that I am writing about now (and forcing myself to talk about now) is the...failure of God to heal my father from dementia. The debilitating illness that robbed my father of his mental faculties. Later in life, I watched it severely impact our family in so many uncomfortable ways. To watch a man so full of life, a man so vibrant, be reduced to not being able to remember the things that once brought him so much joy. A man who reveled in telling rich stories from his childhood, get to the point where those familiar stories were strangers to him. As a boy, he and his siblings were in a singing group.

Some days when he can recall some of the melodies he plays them on the piano. There are some times when he can't remember the words. And then there are other times he'd forget the melody. It became so infuriating to him that eventually, he would stop trying.

His mind was so sharp that he would play Scrabble for hours against himself before this disease robbed him of that intellectual ability. We were on the outside of his mind trying to decipher what else was going on in the prison of his skull. Was he still in there just unable to gather the thoughts, the words to serve him? Or was he not? Was he slipping away right before our eyes, leaving just the shell of his appearance?

And then I'm forced to deal with his occupation and preoccupation with the Ministry. My dad was in ministry all my life. He loved working for the Lord.

To receive a dementia diagnosis is a crappy retirement plan, if I'm being honest. I don't like it. I don't appreciate it.

My mother became his primary caregiver. Her life totally changed. For years during his illness, she had to put up with so much. The entire family changed as we dealt with this cruel disease.

I really don't want to talk about it. It hurts to talk about it. It hurts to remember just how bad it was to live through it. And what sense does it make now that Dad's on the other side, to intentionally dredge up painful memories? It's like poking around in a field of hidden explosives. It doesn't make a lot of sense.

But for now, for whatever reason, I feel this is my calling. It is my mission. I will accept it. I will move in it. I will do the best that I can. Then I will move on.

Where do I start? I don't even know. The first I remember of things starting to change would be coming home and talking to Dad. He would be giving me advice or telling me about something that had happened, and midway through it, he would go into a story that he had told so many times before, that I could finish it for him. And sometimes I did. At times I would interrupt him and say, "Man, you've told that story all my life. I know this story." He would look at me surprised and quickly move on to something else.

Looking back on it now, I wish I had not interrupted him. Oh, what I wouldn't give now to hear him finish one of those stories.

I think there were signs that his mental faculties were starting to diminish. I mentioned it to Mom now and again, but in our community, (and maybe it's not just our community maybe it's our society) we blame it on getting old. "Well, you know, I'm a little older. I don't remember things like I used to," we offer.

That's not what it was.

Mom was taking him to the doctors and I remember getting the news that he had been officially diagnosed with early-onset dementia and it broke me down. I didn't know exactly what dementia was. I had heard about it. You know people went crazy. That's what we called it.

They went crazy. They lost their mind. They were no longer in their right mind. That was not pretty. It was what it was.

But I wasn't aware of it being something that had ever happened to anyone in my family. There were a lot of people who died or passed away from cancer, diabetes, or hypertension, but it was somewhat taboo to have family members who "lost their minds."

So our fears were confirmed that these were not just momentary losses of clarity. There was something much more serious going on. The disease progressed, quickly for some, maybe not quickly for others, but it progressed.

He was able to maintain his job as Pastor for some time because he was still able in some regard to make sound decisions. I guess that clarity would come and go and I suppose there were times when people would question some of his decision-making.

When you've known somebody for years and you love them it's hard to understand what's happening, especially if you don't know about the diagnosis. So eventually it got to a point where something had to be done.

My father was always very active and independent. He would get up in the mornings and go for walks. He would go to the mall where there was a walking club. He was part of The Optimist Club. He was a people person, he loved talking to people. He loved meeting with people.

Some days he would get up early in the morning and be gone. It got to the point where he would get his keys and drive, and we wouldn't know where he was. Sometimes He would go places and get lost.

Dad also began to drive pretty recklessly; until eventually the doctor said he should not be driving at all. They took his license and we had to hide the keys because he would find them.

It was tough watching him lose his independence from doing those things he loved to do. That's when I noticed his entire demeanor begin to change.

He had always been a very gregarious and loving person but as the disease progressed his personality became sour and gruff.

The patience that he had, that he was known for, began to wear thin. My siblings and I would bring our children over to the house. They were young and they were loud. They were kids who didn't get to see each other that much. Of course, they did some things they shouldn't have and he couldn't take it. He would get so angry.

At times his reactions would scare them and us. It got to the point where we had to watch our visits. We had to keep a closer eye on the kids and keep them in spaces where they could be kids and yet not get in his way.

We all knew he absolutely loved his grandkids. To watch that transformation was heartbreaking and traumatic for them, as well.

There was a lot that happened. Some of it I don't want to talk about. Some of it is not mine to talk about. It is what it is.

This is tough.

That's my dad.

What was he like before the sickness? He was my hero. I remember wanting to be like him. I wanted to walk like Dad. I wanted to have Dad's sense of humor, charm, and wit.

We played basketball together. We'd playfully box with each other. He taught me how to cut the grass. He taught me how to chop wood and start a fire in the fireplace. He was a mentor to my friends. He worked in the church diligently, and tirelessly. He took us along with him.

He was a father to those who didn't have a father in their lives. He was very patient with teens. I think that was his calling. Teens of the church felt comfortable talking to him. He was a counselor by profession. So he knew how to do that and he used those skills in his ministry.

After he passed, for weeks we would continue to hear from people who said he was a beacon for them in their lives. I couldn't have been prouder of the man that he was and the man he shaped me to be.

I remember going to the park where he would play basketball games. I longed for the day when I would be old enough to play. He wasn't a big trash talker, but he had fun playing hoops. He liked to let his play do the talking for him. But, of course, he could talk trash, it's part of the game.

He was a sharp dresser. As I grew older we began to wear the same sizes so I raided his closet and borrowed his ties. I don't know how he felt about being able to share his clothes with a teenager. But I felt good about it and it led me to have a love for being able to dress stylishly.

My dad was there for the people around him. I liked the way he took care of business. I liked the way he was always there, but not in a *"see me, look at me this is what I'm doing for you"* kind of way. Rather, he did whatever it was from his heart and in a way that was necessary and appreciated. He did it in a way that did not ask for anything in return. He would do anything for his family.

It was my goal, my wish, to be that kind of father to my children. There was a longing in me, that when I had children there was so much that I was going to be able to share with them. There was so much that I was going to be able to teach them and show them and watch them grow and guide them and mold them into good human beings.

And I'm blessed now to have three children: my oldest Jaydn, my middle child Grant, and my youngest daughter Nia, I love them all so much. And yes, I have been able to do all of those things. I've been able to pour into them.

I remember the early days with Jaydn when I worked nights. During the day before my shift, we would hang out together. We would go fishing or play soccer. On occasion, she would go to work with me. She was my buddy. I was proud of her then and I am proud of her still.

My son was born next. I had always wanted to have a son because there were things that my father shared with me that I looked forward to sharing with him.

After Grant was born, there was a period where he didn't meet certain benchmarks like we thought he would. Shortly after he was born Nia, his baby sister came along. Over time we started noticing that she was progressing in ways that he had not. We went to get him tested and a diagnosis of autism was rendered. That diagnosis tore my wife and me to pieces. This was the son that we had prayed for. We didn't know what autism was. We knew it wasn't fatal. But we knew it wasn't curable. We didn't know what that meant for the kind of life that our son was going to have. We didn't know if he would ever talk. We didn't know the severity of his diagnosis. Autism covers a broad spectrum. It can go from very mild, to very acute cases where children don't speak at all.

Because we didn't know what to expect, we grieved. We came home and sat on the sofa and cried together. That's when I told my wife Sarena, that we could cry for a day but after that, we were going to have to get up, get together, and figure this out. We'd have to figure out what it meant, how to get him help, and what we could expect.

3

Super Duper Daddy Dude

I write for a living. Why is it so hard for me to put these thoughts to paper? Why is it so difficult to recall and record the words that I lived?

Perhaps if I took a 30,000-foot view of the circumstances it would yield better results. I can talk about the issues broadly, but it is when I'm forced to confront them up close that I lose my appetite for entertaining them any further.

Let's try.

Fathers fix things. That's what we do. That's what we attempt to do anyway. We have an innate desire to make it better. Don't know how to ride a bike? Let's learn. Need to fix a hole in the wall? Break out the trowel and some sheet-rock mud. Yard overgrown? Dad's got it covered.

That's what makes us heroes. The fact that our kids can depend on us. That feeling of joy on a kid's face when he brings something broken to his daddy, and somehow his Dad is able to make it all right again...that's a powerful narcotic, that feeling.

There's a time in a kid's life when Dad is the authority on everything. They trust their old man's words wholeheartedly. For a while, Dad wears that badge with pride. He buys into the notion that nothing can stop him from being there for this little human. There is nothing that he can't do for his child, until... Until there is NOTHING he can do for his child.

The realization sets in that he can't do EVERYTHING for his child. Some things the child is going to have to learn to do for himself, like eating solid food, walking, and riding a bike. Dad can't do that for them, but you better believe he's going to be right there beside them showing them how it's done. Until he can't. Until the child doesn't want him there anymore. Until the child says, I've got this. Let me show you.

The first Daddy dilemma. You are fiercely proud of their new-found independence. Your chest swells as they carry out on their own what you have painstakingly taught them to do. But that's the beginning. The beginning of not needing you as much anymore. The beginning of thinking they know the whole playbook when you've only shown them the first few pages.

The Daddy Super Hero cape starts to come off when she rides her bike without training wheels for the first time.

Yes, they still need their father, but the dynamic is different now.

But, what happens when "real life" happens to the child? Not the "they lived happily ever after" life situations, but the ones where doctors don't even have the answers, let alone Daddy.

What does a father do then? What happens when Daddy can't fix it? What happens when everyone is looking to the hero, and the hero is looking to God going, "Hey, a little help with this one!"

What then? What does our "fearless leader" do when his autism-diagnosed son is wreaking holy hell all over the house while Dad's out making a living? Fix that "Super Duper Daddy Dude!" Your daughters don't want to come down to eat because your son can't seem to get his behaviors under control. What does the Daddy manual say about that one?

Discipline. Sometimes that's easier said than done.

What's a Super Duper Daddy Dude to do when he's got no one else to call on, but God and God's not taking any calls right now?

What's the play the Bible recommends running when YOUR only begotten son spits in your face and screams, "Fuck you!" And you, overcome with emotion give it right back to him with a little extra. The punch misses, but the words land on the ears of your daughter who just happened to walk in on your exchange in the dialogue. The word "hypocrite" written in the reflection of the hot tears now rolling down her cheeks.

Or what does our hero do when his adoring wife of 20-plus years hits him with the ultimatum of either the son has to go or she, with our daughters, will. At the time, I worked a late night shift. That left her at home single-handedly trying to protect herself and keep the girls safe from his unpredictable bouts of rage. What do you do when the family that you prayed for and sacrificed for is nearly destroyed by the actions of one of its members? Do you sacrifice the many for the one?

If he were to go someplace, where would it be?

And this is where the words stop flowing as freely. This is the reality of things. As a journalist, I have seen the horror story of what happens to some people in mental health facilities. The abuse and the bad experiences from the other patients and/or staff are enough to rip your heart in two.

I'm not convinced that there are a great many places for an autistic kid to go to get extended behavioral help in South Carolina. Not because they don't exist, but largely because the beds are all full. I was told by doctors in the emergency room that there was nothing they could do for my child. He was too dangerous for us to keep him at home. But since he was not saying that he would harm himself, they weren't going to keep him. There were no beds at the Psychiatric hospital where I thought he could get some help. When I stood my ground and told them he couldn't come back home with me he had to stay there and get some help, I was asked, "Do you want to turn him over to the state Department of Social Services?"

NO. I want him to get help! I'm not giving up on my child. I am begging FOR HELP!!

4

The Emotional Warehouse

Emotions are fragile. My life is too fluid and too dynamic for me to spend a lot of time dealing with emotions. If there is a problem, let's fix the problem and move on. Carefully box up the emotions, push them to the side, and keep it moving. On to the next crisis.

The problem is, that my emotional warehouse is getting full.

There was a bump.

An earth-shattering quake caused my neatly packed boxes of emotion to become jumbled together. Now, it's going to take time and energy that I don't really want to expend to get things back in order.

Some of these boxes are heavy. Some are 30 or more years old. I've gone decades without seeing them or thinking about them. Frankly, I don't know why I'm being forced to deal with them now.

I try to keep the outside of my emotional warehouse immaculate and inviting. There is an anteroom for visitors. It is clean but tiny, with the expectation that those who stop by won't be staying long. Beside the door is a single wooden chair, sturdy but not comfortable.

Beyond that sits the warehouse itself. Boxes and boxes of dusty, musty experiences. Failures, embarrassments, achievements, loves, hurts...you'll find it all here in storage. These are not burdens that I wish to carry around with me daily. And for one reason or another, I'm not exactly free to delete them permanently either. So, here they sit, alone in the dark until something happens, to make me take notice of them.

When that happens I drag the boxes to the EXHUME Room. Sights, smells, sounds, tastes, any feeling is enough to take me there. Freshly cut grass, for instance, takes me back to 5th grade. The scent of the mown clippings from the football field make their way to my upstairs classroom. That smell coupled with all of the emotions of a 10-year old is the passcode to unlocking thousands more long-suppressed thoughts just like it.

But who has time to live in the past like that? Things are happening in the present. As soon as I find what I came here for, I can get back to what's happening now.

As I make my way back to the front door, I notice a thin, yellowed manila folder on the floor. Inside, a single emotional event is scrawled in a 4-year-old's handwriting, labeled "abandonment."

That's funny. I don't ever remember being abandoned. That's because I wasn't. But yet this emotion is real. It is strong. I resonate with it as fully right now, as I did on that day that it DIDN'T happen.

Let me explain. Every day before my Dad went to work he would drop me off at my preschool/daycare. One day as I was pulling up to the school he turned to the back seat, looked at me, and said, "I won't be picking you up today."

He drove off and there I stood, wondering if or when I'd ever see my Dad again.

This was weird. Every day he picked me up after school and took me to Nana's house. What did he mean, "he wasn't going to pick me up?" My mind began to race. There were no big boy beds at the daycare. How was I supposed to sleep here?

I asked my teacher what happens when all the kids are gone. She told me that she cut out the lights and went home. I wondered to myself, what's going to happen to me if no one comes to get me?

THAT was a long and miserable day. I couldn't figure out why my Dad would just leave me. It didn't make any sense. He loved me. We played and did fun things together. Didn't he want me anymore?

I was typically a very happy kid with a broad smile, but not on this day. I wasn't even excited about going to the playground at recess, my absolute favorite part of the day...most days. But not today, because after recess was closer to the time that my Dad "wasn't" going to be there to pick me up.

As my classmates headed for the car rider line to be picked up, my heaviness was noticeable. No one quite knew what was wrong with me. Chris said good-bye and left with his parent. Another friend said, "See you tomorrow."

And then I heard my Mom's voice. They hadn't forgotten about ME!! Someone did want me STILL! I WAS LOVED! Later she would explain to me that my father had a meeting and couldn't pick me up today, but I would see him later. I was relieved.

So why am I now sitting in this warehouse of my feelings choking on tears and snot over this stupid NON-event?!

Because right now as a grown man, those feelings are with me again. I feel exactly that way right now. I'm watching my Dad, my hero, my friend leave me. And again, I feel so abandoned. Daddy, I need you. I need you to tell me what to do. I need you to show me how to raise my son! I need you to see that I'm trying my best to be a good father to my girls and husband to my wife.

Walking in my father's footsteps

Physically my father is still here, but he's been leaving me for years. Dementia has been slowly robbing him of the things that made him, uniquely him. His wit, his charm, his grace, his eloquent speech, and his wisdom are all being siphoned away by this disease. Whereas before he would respond in love and kindness, many times now that's replaced with a gruff order or biting retort. Well-reasoned arguments that he would freely offer up in good-natured debate have been replaced in some cases by shallow nonsense.

For years, he dedicated himself to doing the work of the Lord. He made sure to teach me about God the Father and to walk according to the word. He told me that God would never leave me or forsake me. God, I've asked you to heal my father. Where are you? Why do I feel I'm being abandoned for a third time?

Sometimes I feel like a fatherless child...

You were a great Dad! But I wasn't done needing you! I still need someone I can call. Someone who will reassure me that it's going to be alright. Someone to tell me that he's got my back through it all. Someone to help guide me in raising my son. Except, I don't need SOMEONE I need my Daddy! I'm a grown man with kids of my own and I can't find my DAD!

The metallic clang of something falling to the floor in the back disrupted my thoughts. I pushed through a stack of boxes, and there on the floor in the very back I caught a reflection of the object that had fallen. I'd have to get on my knees and stretch my hands way back there to retrieve it. Almost there...got it!

I am blown away by the discovery. I haven't seen these things in years. I smile. These take me back to when I was eight or nine years old. This is a piece of my dog Butch's collar and ID tag. The memories come gushing back. I really loved that dog!

As a child of the seventies, every little boy wanted a dog as smart as Lassie, as charismatic as Benji, and a pal to get in trouble with like Petey on the Little Rascals. I imagined that if I had a dog we would be best friends like the kids on television and go on endless adventures together.

I begged my parents for a puppy. "I'll remember to feed it and take care of it and clean up after it. I'll take it on walks. Having a dog will make me more responsible," I'm sure I reasoned.

One day they took me to the animal shelter and allowed me to pick out my own dog, a rescue. I scanned the cages and when I saw his black nose and pink tongue I knew this was my guy. A black cocker spaniel mixed with "God knows what". This was the puppy that I wanted. I took him home and named him "Butch". I didn't want a wimpy, whiny dog. I wanted a dog that would be tough. And "Butch" (the bully on The Little Rascals) was the toughest name that I could come up with.

This was what I had dreamed of my whole life. I finally had my own dog like some of my friends. We had a big backyard where we would run around and play. I would create a fort out back and have Butch stand guard to keep out any unwanted guests. I was going to play catch with him and teach him how to fetch, roll over, and shake hands. I couldn't wait to do all of those things. But first, I was going to have to teach him how to go outdoors to use the bathroom. My parents made me clean up his messes. They showed me how to push his face close to the poop and then walk him over to the door to show him where the poop went.

Butch also developed a habit of digging holes in the yard. I guess that's what dogs do, but I had to tell Butch that he couldn't do that here. My bestie also began to wear out his welcome when he began to chew through shoes and other items in the house. This was going to be hard work. Butch also had a bit of a mean streak. Sometimes he would snarl and bark at others. Then there were those times he would get loose in the front yard and we would have to catch him. There was a busy road in front of our house and the last thing I wanted was for Butch to get hit by a car. This particular day the whole family was out in the yard trying to catch him.

"Come back here you old crazy dog!" yelled my Dad.

But Butch kept running. I'd go left, he'd dart right. If Dad zipped, Butch would zag. Even Mom was trying to catch him until her foot slipped into a hole (one probably dug by Butch). She twisted her ankle and fell to the ground in pain.

That was it. When they finally caught Butch, Dad took him back to the pound and that was the last I ever saw of my dog.

I can't believe I kept these tags all of these years. I loved that dog. I cried for days. I was inconsolable. The only thing, outside of my family, that I had ever loved, was gone. My hopes of long walks and mischievous mysteries with my dog would never be. Wow. I guess I still miss you, Butch. There on the floor of my mental warehouse, I began to realize that I have had a more recent experience of these same terrifying feelings. Only this time, it wasn't my dog I was afraid of losing, it was my son.

My only begotten son, whom I had prayed for. The son I was going to teach to throw a ball and ride a bike. The son that I vowed to God that I would care for. I love that kid. But he flies into rages and scares the family. It's okay. I will teach you how to be patient. I don't know what I'm doing, but you're my son and love will find a way. Love will always find a way, right?

"Butch, you can't go running off into the front yard, Ok? You could get in the street and get hit! Don't do that!"

"Son, you've got to stay in control okay? There is a world out there where people are afraid of young black boys. You could get in trouble. Stay in control, OK?"

"Butch, stop digging those holes. Mom doesn't like them. Don't do that!'

"Son, stop punching holes in the walls! That's not what we do. Mom doesn't like that, alright?"

"Butch, please stop making messes. Please! I've done everything I can to help you. You've got to listen to me, they're going to take you away!"

"Grant, son please listen to me. Please calm down. I don't know how to get you to listen to me. I don't want them to take you away!! Please, son! Please!"

5

Talking To Myself

MY INNER CHILD: Why won't you talk to me? Why do you go out of your way to avoid having a conversation with me? I've been sitting by patiently waiting to discuss this, but you keep 'not' finding time to have this talk. It's been years.

ME: I guess I'm just not ready to hear what you have to say.

IC: But you really don't know what I'm going to say. You won't give me a chance.

ME: I know that it's going to hurt. I know that it's going to be painful. It might make me cry or feel weak. Who wants to do that?

IC: So you feel stronger not talking to me about it?

ME: I don't feel weak.

IC: Not talking about it doesn't mean that the pain isn't there. Not talking about it doesn't mean that you're not hurting.

ME: Not talking means I don't have to deal with it right now. You already know the whole story, anyway. We lived it together. Why do you want me to bring all of that back up?

IC: So I don't have to keep carrying it around. This pain is heavy. I'm only eight years old, I'm not built to carry this kind of emotional trauma, year after year after year.

ME: So talk.

IC: Why don't you like me...us...anymore?

ME: It's not that I don't like you. It's just that I should have out-grown you by now. The insecurity, the vulnerability, the not always knowing if I'm making the right decision. The wanting to please my parents and/or God. The feeling of not having the Dad that I knew when I was your age.

IC: But you didn't have a bad life. Most people would agree to that.

ME: I know. And, I don't have a bad life now, but sometimes my feelings and emotions can be overwhelming. I don't have time to deal with such juvenile feelings.

IC: So you shut me out and force me to have to deal with the emotions on my own?

ME: Look, we've already gotten through those moments. They're in the past. There is really no need for me to keep having to think about and relive them. This is so stupid!

IC: So I'm stupid?!

ME: No dummy!! THIS is stupid!

IC: Well, when you're eight years old, you don't really know much of anything about yourself. You go from being carefree to wondering where you fit in the world. When you're eight, you wonder why you're so different from everyone else. Why the other kids seem to know so much about life. You feel like you're an alien who despite his trying, never really fits in. Then when you do fit in a little bit, you're worried every second that everyone will remember, 'Hey look at this guy, he doesn't belong!'

ME: You really weren't all that different from the other kids. You had a different upbringing than some, but overall that was a good thing and it worked out for you in the long run.

IC: Great. You know that, now. You're 51 years old. I'm 8. Remember?

ME: My bad. You know what else I remember about being eight? Taking my imagination out into the backyard and being anywhere and anyone in the world I wanted to be. A motorcycle stunt man, a football player, basketball star, golfer, home run king, explorer, scientist, tree climber, movie star...anything I wanted to be. We were the Backyardigans before the Backyardigans were a thing!

IC: We had a lot of fun. Do you miss it? Ever? being that age?

ME: I don't give myself time to miss it. Can't go back, only forward. Every now and again I might indulge in the luxury of remembering the past, but I've got too much to worry about in the present.

IC: Do you miss, Dad?

ME: What kind of question is that?! Of course, I do. I've missed him for many years now even though he just died a few weeks ago. Dementia robbed us of some deep conversations. I remember Dad when he was the age I am now. I just want to be able to tell him that I admire who he was and what he and Mom did to raise us. The sacrifices that they made, even though I couldn't always appreciate them in the moment. I'm also a little agitated with God for putting me through all of that.

IC: How could you be upset with God?

ME: I had it in my mind, like you do, that God loved me more than anything. I believed that he would hear me if I cried out to him. You couldn't tell me that if I really focused and concentrated on God performing a miracle for me it wouldn't happen. I was convinced. While I was waiting on the miracle, I began to envision what things would look like when he raised Dad from his sickbed and placed him back in the pulpit to preach His word. What a powerful testimony that would be. God LET me believe that. God allowed me to have HOPE that things could be different than what they looked like. Did God just play me? Or did I play myself? Did I just believe the Bible and other preachers and teachers wholesale? I was brought up on faith. I was programmed to believe the Bible. God's word. But when I needed THIS miracle, God let me down.

IC: I don't think I like hearing you say that about God.

ME: I DON'T LIKE IT EITHER!! But what else do you call it? And if I can't count on God to do what I was always taught that He would do, then what does that leave me with? No earthly father and a heavenly father who won't answer me at my most desperate and vulnerable moment. That HURTS. Now I have to make a decision. Is God real? Or is the Bible just a collection of fairy tales for our entertainment? I need a God that I can count on, not one that's going to take away my first superhero. I can't believe Dad is gone and I can't believe that God didn't heal my father. In some ways, I buried my father and at the same time interred my expectations of how I thought God was supposed to respond to my prayers.

IC: Oh.

ME: OH?! Oh. You wanted to talk. Let's talk! Now all you can say is Oh!!!?

IC: But God has been so good to you in so many different ways, even though Daddy is gone.

ME: I know…I know. That's what makes it hard.

IC: So what will you do now?

ME: (sigh) Wait on God to be God again. I have to accept that I can't have everything the way I want it, when I want it. I have to learn to accept that even when things don't appear to be working out for me, they really are. I can't give up on God. Even though my relationship with him may seem strained or strange sometimes, I feel his presence in my life. I see him constantly and every now and then he'll send me a "God hug" so that I can feel him and know that he hasn't forgotten about me. It's just disappointing to know that sometimes when I bring what seems to be a righteous request before him, sometimes he may not see it the same way and may appear to leave me hanging.

IC: How is all of this affecting how you raise your own children?

ME: Honestly, I think about you when I'm raising my kids. They'll do something that I would have done and I'll ask myself, "how would I have wanted my parents to react to this situation?" I'm trying to be patient. I am blessed. God has blessed my family and me in so many wonderful ways. I must trust him in this current season, that he is leading us toward a satisfactory resolution.

IC: How do you feel?

ME: Ok I guess. What do you mean?

IC: Do you feel weak? Did you cry?

ME: Surprisingly, no I don't. And I didn't cry this time.

IC: Thanks for talking to me.

ME: No problem. But I've got one request.

IC: What is it?

ME: Can we stop having these conversations at 5 am?

6

Jesus Walks

I usually don't remember my dreams, but this one was so odd I couldn't shake it. I remember standing along the side of a road with a throng of other people waiting for Jesus to come by. We were a few yards away from where he was and I was so excited to get to introduce him to Grant. The crowd was mesmerized. Every few feet he would stop and touch someone and they would be healed. Joy welled up inside of me because I knew in just a few moments Jesus was going to heal my boy, just like he performed healing miracles in the bible.

I can see the smile on his face, we're next! I can't believe it!

"Hi Jesus, this is my son Grant!" I exclaim.

He smiles down at Grant then looks up at me and says, "He has autism," and continues to walk down the line.

I am befuddled by what just happened here. I think to myself, yes he has autism that's why I brought him here. But I said nothing, and Jesus walked away.

7

"The Autism Whisperer"

Since my son was diagnosed with autism, I find myself wanting to help when I am around people with special needs. I have the desire to be a bit more patient...a bit more empathetic. The Caesar Milan of the autism community.

Caesar Milan is known as "The Dog Whisperer". His television show highlighted his keen love and dedication to the animals. He connected with them, and they to him.

Now relax, I'm not trying to compare people on the spectrum or those with special needs to dogs. But the quality that I admire is Milan's ability to recognize what the canine wants and needs and communicate with it to achieve the desired results.

I've poured through several episodes carefully attempting to find his secret sauce. What's the magic language that he's using to communicate? It appears that his biggest tools are psychological. Why is the animal behaving in this way? What is causing it to be unfulfilled? How can I meet its needs and bring about the desired behavior?

I attempted to apply what I learned from watching the show to my son. What is he not saying that is causing him to behave in this manner? What is the underlying cause of this behavior? How can I get him to a calm state so that he can talk to me about whatever is going on in his head?

Before long it occurred to me that I was going to have to develop different strategies to get him to a state of calm. Going bigger than his meltdowns was not as effective a way of getting to the root cause of them. Being offended by the behavior was equally counterproductive. Grabbing him while he was raging out, proved to bring about more harm than good. He didn't want to be restrained and he was misinterpreting my approach, as me being combative. All of those methods proved to be the equivalent of pouring gasoline on a fire. They made things 100 times worse.

Before I could help my son through one of his emotion-filled episodes, I realized that I first had to deal with my own issues. I had to come to grips with the fact that each time he "wilded out" I was weighing myself on the parent scale and coming up lacking each and every time.

My child won't listen to me. What am I doing wrong?

When I was young and my parents told me to "knock it off" I knocked it off! (At least that's the way I remember it.) On the occasion that I was being really thick-headed, they may have resorted to corporal punishment to reinforce their request. I generally got the message after that.

However, when I would attempt to apply my parents' behavioral techniques to my son, they generally didn't have the desired impact. Which led me to ask, "What am I doing wrong?"

From time to time, in my adolescent years, my mother would threaten to take me out to the regional mental hospital or the youth detention center if I didn't improve my behavior. She would warn that if I didn't change my ways that is where I would wind up.

So I thought, maybe I will try this approach with my son. But to do so, I first had to explain to him what those institutions were. I had to paint them as places he did not want to go. This scared-straight approach worked to limited effect. But I now realize that I planted a negative stigma in him towards places that are designed to offer help. That's not good. And when we eventually had to resort to sending him to one of these places, both of us felt a sense of failure and shame.

Grant was not my parents' son, he was mine. Despite feeling that I had been blessed with the best parents on the earth, I had to realize that not every tactic that worked with me, would work on my boy.

My father was a high school guidance counselor. I would hear from people all over the county about how much my Dad offered them sound wisdom and advice when they were going through the worst parts of their lives. They told me how he had listened to them non-judgmentally as they explained their trouble. I was jealous of that. I didn't feel I had someone to talk to the way they did. Sure there were Dad's counselor friends that I could have reached out to, but I was pretty certain that they would have gone back and told him everything I said. I didn't really feel that I had that safe space.

And yet, my Dad was awesome. He was a good father. I could and did go to him and talk about some things. But when I felt I needed someone to just listen to me and not judge what I had done, but help me process through it, I didn't get that from him. Looking back on it from this side of parenthood, he probably felt a certain level of fear himself. Like, "I've helped all of these other kids, but I can't stop my own son from being a knucklehead." He had worked at school all day, and when he came home he was in Dad mode. Another retrospective that I imagine he carried from hearing the problems of other teens, was that he needed to be harder on his own child so that he (I) wouldn't be faced with the same challenges that came through his office. Either way, I respect it.

Eventually, I concluded that to be the best Dad I could be to my son, Grant, I was going to have to be his counselor first. In fits of rage, I had to put the fire out, before I began fathering him. Then after the fire was out we had to sit together in the midst of the dying embers and talk about what had just happened and develop strategies to prevent things from getting this bad the next time.

Previously, I had rejected this namby-pamby approach to parenting. I was deadset against raising weak children. They have to learn that there are consequences to their actions. I'm not going to be the kind of parent who just lets my kids get away with everything. They will have discipline. They will know structure!

THAT is how a STRONG parent raises their kids, I thought. THAT is GOOD PARENTING, I thought. THAT is what's going to make my parents proud of the parent that I have become. But will THAT make my child proud of the person that I have become?

Honesty required me to have a one-on-one conversation with myself. Have you adopted these beliefs because you truly believe in them? Or have you adopted these beliefs and strategies because that's all you know? Are these the best tactics for your kids or are these the tactics that were good enough for you?

Trying to fit the parenting mold that I thought society and my parents had poured for me was absolutely NOT working for me. I would have to be brave enough to try to find something that worked for my child and my situation. Even if that something went against EVERY-THING that I thought went into making a good parent.

8

Imagination vs Faith

When my sister and I were younger we shared a bedroom. When we were supposed to be going to sleep we would lie in bed entertaining each other with made-up stories about a make-believe place, Dreamland.

We'd say,

"I'm going to Dreamland!"

"Me too! Did you see that fat lady last night?!

"Yes" retorted the other, "she tried to go down the glass slide!"

We convinced ourselves that when we went to sleep we were dreaming the same dream. Even though as we sat awake we were making up the whole thing.

Sometimes though, she would have me convinced that she really saw those things. Then I would add to her account of what had happened in this magical make-believe place.

We were co-creators and co-curators of our own imaginary world. It didn't matter that both of us were lying, that was the fun of it. The goal was to see how grand we could make this fantastical fiction.

Years later I remember feeling that way again, in church. All of these people are telling the same fantastical story about a savior and what he had done for them. How they could feel him, all over them. I didn't feel anything, but I played along and wondered if I was participating in a grown-up version of Dreamland.

Relax. I know there is a God. At least, I believe that there is. I've had too many encounters with Him to think otherwise. But my stories and experiences with Him are real. Not made up, like dreamland.

But even so, how do I know that He will do what "His Word" says He's going to do? I've taken him at "His word" before and those prayers were interred with the loved one I was desperately believing in Him to save.

So I stopped believing in "supernatural" miracles and settled for "run of the mill" miracles.

"Hey! I found $6 on the street!"

I started looking for those "ain't God good" kind of miracles. I'll just toss God some problems that He can handle, nothing too big, just enough for me to hold on to my belief that you "love me" and that you exist.

9

"Trust Issues"

Dear God,
   I believe in you! Isn't that enough? Why do you need me to trust you too? That's asking a lot!

Why can't you be satiated with my romantic notion of your greatness? Why is my adoration and praise not enough?

Despite, what others think, I believe. No matter what others say, their words don't sway me. I might not be able to persuade them to see you the way I do, but they can't persuade me to see you differently, either.

It really is a good setup, please don't go and mess it all up...asking me to trust you!

Here's the deal! I've believed in you in times past. I've believed that you could or would do a thing...and you didn't. If I get to the point where I'm TRUSTING you and you don't perform (i.e leave me hanging again) then what do I have left?

NOTHING. NO THING. Not a thing to believe in. I'm just not ready to be hopeless. If I believe in you there's hope that you'll come through. If you don't ...I have nothing. You are my last card. I save you for the impossible. You are my 'In case of fire break glass'. I'm afraid to fully trust you because what if you're not behind the glass? What if I'm only left to gather shards? Then my last card would have been for naught. NO! Please let me keep my belief intact. It's easier to believe than to trust.

Belief is like a flashlight beam cutting through darkness. I aim my "belief" in the direction of my attention and watch as it illuminates the unknown future. I think it's going to work out. I hope it's going to work out. I've got it pointed in the right direction, let's see what happens.

Trust? Now that requires a commitment. Trust is standing on stage in front of the crowd and being asked to choose which door contains the prize. You make your choice, then have a seat...unbothered. Trust is unaffected by the dramatic music and tense drum beats that build. Trust is actually annoyed that you're going through all of these theatrics to try and make IT nervous when you know good and well your prize is behind curtain number _____!

But that's trust. How can we move to trust when there have been times my belief went unrewarded? You expect trust, when the next best thing, my beliefs, have been heartbroken numerous times? How does that work?

Seriously. How does that work?

On my job, I don't get a promotion until I show mastery of the first level. You want an upgrade of TRUST in this relationship when you don't even have the courtesy to appreciate the effort it takes to *believe* in you?!

There is no one and no thing I believe in more than you. I give you my belief. My trust is more valuable. More precious. My Trust is like my heart. If I gift it to you and you abuse it, I have nothing. I am nothing. I existed for nothing. I spent my life in a scam. I bet on the wrong color.

If I give you my TRUST what guarantees can you give me that you won't abuse it? How do I know you'll take better care for IT, than you did with my belief?

Belief is shooting the basketball at the rim and thinking it will go in.

Trust is turning your back to the basket, closing your eyes throwing up the shot as the clock reaches zero, and walking to the locker room because you know intuitively without looking that you've just hit the game-winning shot!

Are you worthy of my trust?

Belief says, "This might work." Trust says, "It's DEFINITELY going to work!" I can actively participate in my belief system. But when I trust, all control of the situation is removed from my hands.

I was at the pool with my kids and I was trying to teach my youngest daughter to float on her back. To let the water hold her up. I placed my hands underneath her back and told her to relax. As long as she felt my hand she was fine. My hand wasn't really holding her, it was just there. The moment I slowly let it down, she stiffened and began to sink.

That's how I feel.

There's a saying, "Fool me once, shame on you. Fool me twice, shame on me!" That's what this feels like. You've had multiple chances with my beliefs and you fumbled the ball. Why should I trust you, with my TRUST?

God, you made me to desire a certain amount of independence. But you've made it where my independence only gets me so far. You are my father. You are great and all-powerful.

I don't mind trusting you. But sometimes you don't come through in the way that I requested. That stresses me out. I feel like you will have my back, but all indications sometimes suggest that you will not.

If I'm delivered from my predicament in a way that is not obviously your doing, I tend to feel as if you didn't come through. I wonder if you are angry with me. Did I do something that I should not have done? Is this my punishment?

Love always,

Raphael

10

"Press My Way On"

I'm *gonna press my, press my way on, anyhow.*
I'm gonna press my, press my way on, anyhow.
It matters not, what the people say.
They wanna make me,
they wanna make me,
make me, stop and turn around.
But I'm gonna press my,
press my way on, anyhow.

I can't stop singing this song and crying today.

As angry and hurt as I am by you sometimes God, the truth is, I can't stop trusting you, I can't stop leaning on you, I can't stop pressing my way on. I just can't. And you know it.

You've got me just where you want me, vulnerable. Broken.

11

"God, this is some BS!"

God, you know this is some bullshit! My father lived his whole life for you. He deprived himself of family time so that he could do what you had him do. He lived a life of service to others, in your name. And this is how you let it go down. You strip the dignity of the man's character through a mind-robbing illness? What the hell is this about?

And my son?! I only ever wanted to have a son so that I could share with him the things that my Dad taught me. I wanted to be there for him. You allow my son to have autism? I get that maybe I haven't lived the perfect life. But what did my son ever do to you? Please don't punish him for my screw-ups.

And the thing about it is this, my dad, and my son, are beautiful souls. How could you? Why would you?

Do you ever wonder why people don't trust you? Things like this don't help. The Bible is full of examples of miracles being performed. I have BEEN waiting on miracles. I have always believed that you hold the power to heal them both. I still believe it. I'm waiting on you. What's the hold-up?

And while we're talking about the Bible and trust, I never did really appreciate that whole Job story. It never set well with me. Another dude who is living life, by all accounts, for your glory. You're sitting around talking to the Devil and poof! Just like that, you blow up Job's spot! You kill his kids and afflict him with sores. Why? To prove a point to the DEVIL? Who is HE, that you have to prove anything to him AND at poor Job's expense! And this really ticked me off, at the end of his story Job is whole, healthy, wealthy, and with a new family. Well, I'll be damned! What kind of story is this?! It's not the story of a God of love. This is one book that keeps me from believing that the Bible is the ultimate word of God. This book makes me lean towards the Bible just being a collection of stories.

A God of love wouldn't do that. A righteous God wouldn't allow that. How can I trust a God who says, 'he loves me', but allows these kinds of things to happen against my desperate cries for help?

Are you just screwing with me right now like you messed with Job? I don't know why. I'm not nearly as noble as Job. Everyone who loves my son and father is hurting as a result of these calamities that you have allowed to befall my family.

Since the beginning, as YOU are my witness, I have prayed to you for a miracle. I have believed against hope that the miracle was well within your power to perform. Any second now, things will turn around. Won't they?

I was taught to love you...to fear you...to reverence you. My childhood pastor, Elder Cleveland Wood, was the closest representative I could find on earth of what you must be like. He was always kind. He was full of wisdom. He loved you. He was like a grandfather. He was easy to love. I wanted to do nice things for him, like carry his briefcase, or hold the door open for him. If I were misbehaving, when he came around I would straighten up. He was the spiritual leader of our church flock. I imagined you to be Elder Wood, to the 100th power!

Now as a man, I'm struggling to know who you are. Are you a God of love who loves me no matter what? Who wants to see me prosper more than anything? Or are you the Old Testament God who gets his rocks off making deals with the devil about how much he's allowed to torment those of your children who love and revere you the most?

Or are you that angry God who calls on your "chosen people" to utterly wipe another group of humans from the face of the earth?

Women, babies, cattle, everything, everyone must go. Is that who you are? With a handful of storms, you send death and destruction to the nations in the form of hurricanes, fires, earthquakes...ACTS of God! Again, tell me why it was necessary for a group of humans, that you created, to physically destroy another nation of people that you created.

Am I angry at you? Or am I angry at myself for so readily believing in you? For wanting to believe that the Bible stories were true. For wanting to believe that someone bigger than me was capable of loving me. That's right, your son Jesus. You loved me so much that you sent him to die. Ooooohkay. Wow.

You asked me if I trusted you. I don't even know who you are anymore. I so desperately need to believe in you the way I did when I was a kid. When you had the characteristics and love of my Pastor. And would never think of allowing those kinds of hurts and pains to endure in my life...especially after I've asked my almighty Father for help. I need more than childish songs that say you love me *"for the Bible tells me so."* I need YOU to tell me so.

Heal my Dad, God. Heal my son. In Jesus' name. Amen.

12

The Church of My Youth

I pull up to the parking lot of my childhood church and start to cry. Through the tears, I can see much clearer the reason behind the argument with my wife the night before. I'm forced to concede, it wasn't a miscommunication issue after all. I just don't want to be here.

This church was the epicenter of my life, growing up. There wasn't a week that went by that this building and these people were not a part of it. The church is much older than I am, but this building...I helped build it! I was there when the foundation was laid. When the walls were framed. When the sheetrock went up. I was connected to every aspect of it.

I watched my father go from youth leader to assistant pastor to pastor. I served on the choir and usher board. I got saved in this church, every summer during the youth revival!

This is the church where I met my wife. Where I made friends for life. This house of worship prayed us through afflictions. This body of believers joined faith with my wife and me when the doctor said we couldn't have children. Then they rejoiced with us at each child's dedication service.

Within these walls, I became acquainted with gut-wrenching grief. The children's choir sang at the double funeral here of two young boys who accidentally drowned.

The words of my father's sermons, I believe are still reverberating somewhere in the rafters. His blood, sweat, and tears, his life work poured into this building...this family of believers.

I reminisce on what was, as I realize what is. Another pastor's name is on the marquee now. Another man's vision is being enacted, while my father sits there, in the pulpit, asleep. Oblivious to the changes going on around him. He's got more than 50 years of equity invested in "The Lord's Work" and THIS is his retirement package?

So I sit in the car and let the tears come. Not realizing that I'd need them back a few hours later.

Several weeks prior my firstborn went to the altar to ask for a miracle concerning her grandfather's health.

Let that sink in. My firstborn. My oldest daughter. The child that doctors said we couldn't have when my wife got sick. "Your body is serving as its own birth control right now", is what they told my wife. The daughter that this church helped us pray into existence.

The mothers and missionaries helped us bombard heaven with prayer. We touched and agreed. We fasted, and despite what it looked like "God heard" our pleas and gave us our miracle.

Now, our miracle is asking heaven for a miracle of her own. She has believed in the power of prayer and the awesomeness of God. Of her own volition, she stepped into the aisle and asked the minister to pray with her that her grandfather's health be restored.

The minister's response was, "What if God doesn't heal your grandfather? Can I pray for your peace instead?"

What???

"I don't think healing your grandfather is in God's plan so I'll pray for you to have peace instead."

Whoa!

Eventually, I was able to talk to that minister face to face. He repeated exactly the same thing to me that he told my daughter. He looked me in my face and said God told him that my father would not be healed. That he would leave here with Alzheimer's.

I said even if that is so (I don't accept it or believe it) what's the harm in praying the prayer that you were asked to pray in faith?

His reply was that he didn't want to pray against the will of God. If God had already determined this fate for my father, he wouldn't offer a prayer that was counter to His will.

In the bible, the prophet told King Hezekiah that he was going to die. Hezekiah petitioned God and the prophet had to come back and tell him that God had heard his prayer and that he would live. So, there is biblical precedence for God changing his mind.

We talked for quite a while, the minister would not relent. He ended the conversation with, "Well let's see who's right then."

The most hurtful part about this exchange for me is my father greatly poured into this minister's life. When I was a child, I remember how much this minister looked up to my Dad. My father invited him and others over to play basketball. He talked about how much he admired my father. And now that my Dad is older he can't be bothered to pray a prayer for his healing because God has already told him it's not going to happen?!

If God told me someone I loved was not going to be healed I wouldn't stop asking him to please reconsider. And here's the thing minister...I don't care about being right or proving you wrong. I just want my Daddy back.

13

Grace

He really didn't deserve this.

All my life, my Dad had modeled appropriate, godly behavior. His name in the community was good. He was well-respected and admired. It must have taken everything out of him to come and bail his oldest son out of jail.

The night before, what I can remember of it, I had gone to a party. It was full of alcohol and people I didn't know. Friends of friends. The rest of my recollections from that night are blurry, at best. I don't exactly remember what happened. Maybe I've just blocked it out so I don't have to deal with the embarrassment of it.

What I do remember is sitting shirtless in the back of a squad car on my way to jail, charged with public intoxication. It was a sobering ride, as I contemplated how this was going to affect my life.

Up til that point, and never since, had I ever been that wasted. I don't believe it was only alcohol. I can't prove it, but I think I may have been drugged. Either way, that doesn't change the fact that I voluntarily participated in activity that I knew was wrong.

As I was placed into the holding cell with others who "hadn't done anything wrong", I could feel the world laughing at me. Judging me. Pointing fingers at the fool. What a jackass.

Some years before that, I made conscious decisions to chase after cool. I saw myself as tremendously uncool. Unpopular. The me, that I saw, wasn't quite enough. Not good-looking enough, not athletic enough, not smart enough, not popular enough. I was a church boy because that's what my parents had made me. I determined that every chance I got, I would systematically shed that image and renovate my personality.

What were my parents trying to keep me from? What was life like on the other side? Why couldn't I just be normal? I didn't want to stand out as much as I just wanted to blend in. This was my life. I said to myself, "My parents may not approve, but I'm going to find out what life is about on the other side and create myself in my own image, of what I want to be."

In hindsight, getting arrested that night may have saved my life...or someone else's. I was in no condition to drive, but I may have tried to anyway. When I called my Dad, I wasn't really sure he would come and get me. He had warned me about the lifestyle I was chasing. But I didn't listen. It was Sunday morning, by now. After bailing me out, he then had to go to the church he pastored and bring the sermon.

He didn't deserve that.

I tried so hard to avoid living the life that had been set before me. It seemed so boring, so bland, so not like what I wanted. I didn't have ambitions of being a renegade. I didn't want to be an addict or a drunk. I didn't want to live a totally Godless life. I wanted the freedom to choose. I felt God was forced on me, so I rejected and resented religion.

Inside of the church I had been accepted and loved. Outside of the church, I felt I was a fish out of water. I couldn't relate in many ways to my peers. I was ridiculed for it.

I spent the rest of my life in social "remediation" classes trying my darndest to catch up. By the time I caught up, I realized that I had overshot my mark. Now, I was doing things that were a step too far, for those peers I'd been trying to impress. I was sliding into dark places and didn't know how to come back.

Mom and Dad would have been within their rights to kick me out and let me figure it out on my own. But they didn't.

Though I have come a long way with my life and choices, I still feel pain for the heartache that I caused them. I've not quite been able to tell myself that it's OK, even though my parents have continuously shown me love. It's hard for me to forgive myself now for causing the ones I love, so much needless heartbreak.

I'm sorry.

But parenting is payback. Sometimes I can't understand why my children won't listen. If they would just do what I say their lives would be so much easier. And I've got GOOD kids.

More ironic still though are the episodes that I've watched my father go through on numerous occasions.

In one stage of his diagnosis, he became mean and gruff with others. A disposition that couldn't be farther from his true character.

My Dad never met strangers. He could carry on a conversation with anyone. He was a "people person" and very comfortable in his own skin. He was kind, courteous, and polite.

When I began to see him display this odd behavior, it was alarming. I scolded him. I apologized profusely to others on his behalf. I was mortified at this bizarre transformation. I was ashamed. I couldn't believe he was acting like this...except he had a medical diagnosis behind his behavior. I did not.

I know I put my parents through a lot. I regret it now looking back on situations where I was just hardheaded and rebellious. I was living my life the way I wanted to live my life. I didn't want to be placed in their constraints. They had chosen their path and I wanted to be free to choose my own.

The problem is I didn't know what I wanted to do or be. I just knew what I didn't want to be, at least not right then. I made mistakes. Lots of them. I would come to find out later, that I needed my parents a lot more than I previously thought.

As I became frustrated with the outcomes of my own actions, I slowly began to be brought back into the lessons of my youth. I began to see that perhaps I could still maintain my freedom to be a "me" that I previously could not even imagine. Eventually, the prayers of my parents were heard and answered. To their relief and delight, I matured and became a responsible adult. My parents beamed at each success and achievement. My sins of the past were forgiven and mostly forgotten.

Fast forward. I am married to the woman of my dreams. The woman who helped me to grow up and realize that I didn't have to try and fit someone else's mold of who I should be. She helped me find my true self. When I took off all the masks, she didn't run away. She appreciated the "Me" that I was trying to shield from the world. We fell in love got married and had three beautiful children. It was my goal to bring them up to be good responsible adults and show them early on that they were enough.

I received much grace in my formative years, and now that I had children of my own, Grace showed up with an invoice. The itemized bill was shown to me every time one of my darling children didn't do what their mother and I asked of them. Each time they did something so amazingly, incredibly dumb, there was Grace, daring me to get upset about it.

Ironically, it was my son's bout with mental health challenges that threatened my own sanity. In our interactions, logic and reason were foreign concepts. My child's actions made no sense, and despite my best efforts, I couldn't rationally make him aware of his errors.

Physical punishment was like throwing water on a grease fire, the results were disastrous. I thought I was patient. I tried everything. I talked to my parents who were sympathetic but reminded me of the troubles they had with a certain young man many years ago. They encouraged me to stay the course. They told me that I was doing everything right and to trust God.

After an eternity of running up against a brick wall, it dawned on me that I would have to change my tactics or go crazy. It was a very difficult pill to swallow. My parents were old school. They didn't tolerate disrespect and I'd be doggone if I was going to allow one of my children to disrespect me, in my house.

I had seen children run all over their parents in public and had vowed that, that would never be my kids. I'd seen kids curse their parents out and throw temper tantrums and thought, my kid would have a bloody lip if they tried that with me. I surmised that "those kids had not been taught proper respect and lacked home training".

But what had been effective at 'controlling me' as a child, had not always been effective with my own offspring. I was at a crossroads.

The question I had to ask myself was this, "Do you want to actually BE a good parent? or do you want EVERYONE else to THINK that you are one? My child needed me to figure this out.

I decided that I was not my parents, and my child was not me. If I were going to be successful at raising this human I would have to approach them human to human on a level plane. I was still the parent, but it was so imperative for me to present myself to them with a level of equal respect, not as Daddy all the time.

Each of my children has a different personality. They have different strengths and weaknesses. They have different motivations. A parent who doesn't understand the differences and how to work within the framework of those characteristics, I feel, is setting themselves up for undue heartache.

I learned that when I sat and talked with them, I got better behavioral results. When I stopped screaming, they stopped screaming. When I stopped reminding them of how stupid the thing they did was, they began to listen to me. When the topic of correction centered around how this would make them better, instead of how crappy it made me feel when they did this action, light bulbs came on.

It was not a quick or easy process but it was **so** rewarding. By calmly talking about the issues (once "peace" has been re-established)

I can listen to their rationale. I can begin to see their thought process (even though I don't fully understand it). I stopped being judgmental and they stopped feeling so judged. The Bible is right in that a "soft answer turneth away wrath." And in those moments when my child feels comfortable enough to talk to me knowing that I STILL love them fully, miracles have happened. A tiny phrase is released from them that becomes the key to another much-needed dialogue.

That's Grace.

If you have been given grace, you must show grace.

14

"Grant James! Grant, Grant, James!"

Somewhere I read that breathing and meditation can help change your disposition. Breathe in deeply. Hold it. Exhale. Innnnnnnnn...Outttttt.

Through practice, I have found the repetition and the cleansing of each breath does yield a calmer state. The action of it allows the dark moody clouds to roll away.

By inhaling the clean crisp air around me I was able to push out the repressive toxic air within. Innnnnnnn...Outttttt.

Hanging in the air in front of my face dissipating into microscopic molecules was everything that frustrated me about my child. His inability to do what I say or downright defiance of my wishes...drifting away on the winds. The frustration of not being able to control the actions of a special needs child was drawn from my belly and pushed out into the universe through my lips. There's more room for that toxicity out here than in there.

I'm not a smoker, but that's what this feels like. I'm going to take one more deep, slow drag off of this meditation and then expel my fears, doubts, and insecurities that this moment has caused.

Now that my head is clear from that funky fog, I can try to focus on what I can do to be a more effective parent. It feels as if I've tried it all. I've exercised EXTREME patience. I've been the drill sergeant.

I've tried being his friend (THE last thing a black parent would ever recommend). I've tried spanking. I've tried time-outs, restrictions, grounding, and different variations of all of the above and in this moment...none of it is working.

To his credit, he doesn't like being this way. There seem to be only two modes for him lately. There's calm and FREAK THE FREAK OUT!! Usually, the meltdown is over something he can't find. A sock, his tablet, the mouse to his computer, a stuffed animal he hasn't seen or played with in three years but NOW he has to know where it is. And then once you drop everything to help him find it...he's cool. He doesn't want the teddy bear! Nope. Just wanted to know where it was!

So one particular morning, we had gone at it about something. There was a huge crisis for him and the incessant whining began. I AM FIRECRACKER HOT! I let him have it. WE GO IN! I tell him he's too old to be acting this way!

Shortly afterward, whatever had caused the episode, was over and just like that...he was fine. I on the other hand was not! This little unnecessary scene had gotten my pressure up.

"I'm sick of this! It has to end!" I mean, I am FURIOUS!

A few moments later he comes up to me smiling (keep in mind, for him, it's over. He's cool and in his mind, I should be too!).

He says, "Daddy, tell me 'Go, Grant James, Grant, Grant James!'"

A NO the size of Stone Mountain, Georgia rose up from the tips of my toes, rushed through my entire central nervous system at the speed of light, and would have exploded out of my mouth...but it got stuck in the back of my throat.

The creases in my face ready to ride the waves of the NOOOO that was most assuredly coming; instead turned into lines of confusion.

Before me stood my son, who moments ago had behaved in a manner that I detested. This same son, now had the audacity to ask me to bestow upon him a generous dose of positive praise?!

Are you kidding me? Are you serious right now?

He was.

There was a light in his eye and a smile in his heart as he asked me to lift him up...encourage him...and raise his self-esteem.

My instincts said, "Heck no!" but in the same second the father in me said, "Heck yeah!"

* * *

Several weeks before this incident in a moment of divine clarity, the idea hit me that it would be a good idea for Grant and me to work out together when he would become "stuck".

That's the word I use when his behavior begins to shift. He was fine one moment and the next you could sense the onset of a meltdown approaching. When this happens we know that a total breakdown is imminent, in most cases it's about three seconds away.

I've found that if we can work up a sweat or produce enough tears and snot, those toxins that caused him to become anxious or agitated, leave through those fluids. It generally works pretty well and there's the added benefit of exercise.

So, as I had him jogging the neighborhood, I noticed the anger buildup dissipating. He was no longer struggling with his behavior, but he was struggling to keep up the pace.

My anger subsided. This guy is my son. He's a good kid who has trouble with emotional outbursts. But he's a great kid. My heart softened, not enough to END the run, but enough to encourage him that HE could make it.

In the military, during our physical training, we would run and someone would call cadence. The leader would cry out and the troops would repeat the refrain. It was a technique to get us all going in the same direction, at the same speed, to the same beat. Calling cadence took some of the struggles out of the run.

"Let's GO son", I thundered.

"Who's the best kid in the whole wide world? Grant James. Grant, Grant James!"

"Who respects every man, woman, boy or girl? Grant James, Grant, Grant James!"

He looked back at me surprised, but it was obvious he liked it. I smacked him on the butt and yelled, "LET'S GO SON!"

"This kid is a genius and he's nice to all! Grant James, Grant, Grant James!" I hollered.

He had found another gear now! Smiling all the way. By the time we were finished with our run around the block, he was singing his own song with fresh fervor. I had my son back.

* * *

Fast forward to today. Fast forward to his request. Now journey with me through the synapses of my brain as that question is processed through a field of neurons and electrons.

"You want me to validate you after you behaved so badly? You want me to encourage you and make you feel good about yourself, even though right now you've got me feeling like crap? YOU WANT ME to override my anger and negativity and come up with positive affirmations about you?!", I asked in my mind.

His eyes smiled back, "Yes please, Daddy."

The nerve of this guy!

I choked on that big fat NO in the back of my throat and returned it to the bottom of my toes. I swallowed a lump of pride and came up with,

"He's a very smart guy and always distinguished, Grant James, Grant, Grant James!"

15

"When The Mountain Doesn't Move"

The father, the son, and the son's son

Sarena James, photo credit

The father loves his son because his father loved him. The father is hurt because his son is not acting the way he has been taught to act. The father is angry at the son. The father is worried about the son. The father is scared for the son.

The father refuses to give up on the son.

Eventually, the son comes around and begins to make better decisions.

The father is proud of the son.

The son becomes a father.

The son's father couldn't be happier.

The son's son is diagnosed with autism.

The son is devastated. The father consoles him.

The father calls him a good man and a good father.

The son feels encouraged by his father's words.

The father says it's going to be all right.

The father becomes old and is diagnosed with dementia.

The son is very sad because he loves his father.

The son hates seeing his father this way.

The father begins to not remember.

The father tells stories that the son has heard his entire life as if he's telling them for the first time.

The son feels hopeless.

The father begins acting in ways that disagree with his character.

The father is more childlike. At times displaying a rough and harsh demeanor.

The son chastises the father. The son is angry at the father. The son is worried about the father. The son is scared for the father.

The son refuses to give up on the father. He determines that he will have faith for a different outcome. He will not lose faith.

The father's health and mental health is in decline.

The grandson's mental health is in decline.

The son feels overwhelmed. He can't figure out why things aren't changing. He doesn't know what to do to get a different outcome.

Ordinarily, he would go to his father for help. But his father has been gone for some time now, even though he's still alive.

His father taught him to talk to his heavenly father, which he does regularly.

However, he's not getting the answers that he wants to get.

What happens when you have mustard seed-sized faith and the mountain still doesn't move?

16

Saltwater Spit Shine

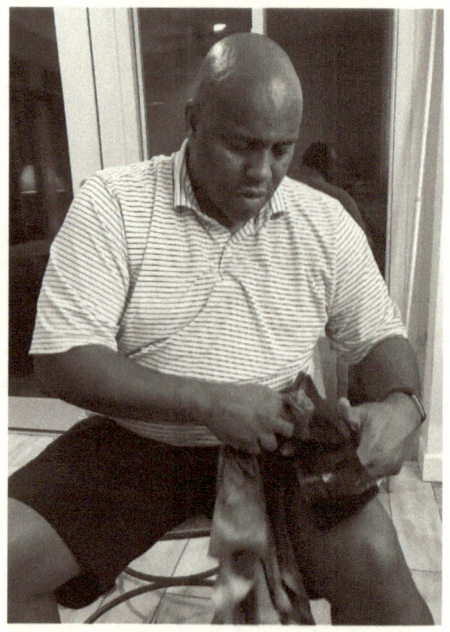

Sarena James, photo credit

"Come here, Raphael. It's time for you to learn to shine your own shoes."

It was Saturday night. We were winding down for the night. I was around eight years old. My Dad brought out the shoe-shine kit. A brown box, a tattered old t-shirt with shoe polish all over it, and a thick brush. The rag was almost completely covered in brown and black shoe polish.

He wiped the shoe then whisked over it with a brush. Then he told me to put my fingers on the disgusting rag. There was no CLEAN place to touch it. There was no way I was going to get out of this without getting dirty.

I watched him put polish on his cloth and place it all over the shoe. I thought, "Uh-oh, Daddy are you sure that's the shoe polish?"

The glob of polish had turned the shoe hideously dull. Every inch of the leather he covered had taken what little sheen the shoes had, away.

Then he took the brush and went to town on that shoe. With the precision of a madman, he went back and forth across that leather until the dull gave way to a reluctant shine. I was shocked and amazed. Then he took another old t-shirt (slightly less covered in polish) and began buffing the toe. He would talk to me and tell me stories of spit-shining his shoes in the Army.

"SPIT on shoes?!" I was intrigued. "Please tell me more", my inquisitive eyes signaled.

He showed me how to put a little spit onto the shoe and work it into the polish in short circles until the leather turned to glass. It was amazing!

A few days ago, my mother (my father's caretaker) texted my siblings and me. The tone was serious. My Dad's health had deteriorated to the point that he needed round-the-clock care. And she was his 24/7 nurse. Things had become overwhelming and she needed help.

We all promised her that we would step up our efforts. I knew that she had a lot on her plate, but she never shared with us exactly how taxing his care could be.

We came down for a visit and she made a list of things we could do to help her out. We jumped on it. One thing she asked me to do...polish Dad's shoes.

"Come here, Grant," I called out to my son, "I'm going to show you how to polish shoes."

With Dad looking on in the background I helped Grant find a place on that remarkably dirty shoe polish-filled cloth and walked him through the process of shining shoes.

He really wasn't all that interested...or impressed. Come to think of it, maybe I wasn't all that excited at being presented with another chore at that age, either.

But in this moment, looking at those shoes, my heart got to remember my hero teaching me one skill set that would aid in my becoming a man.

I dismissed Grant after we did the first shoe together. I looked at my Dad, then back down to the shoe and I went to town. For some reason, the shoes (my Dad's shoes) weren't shining enough. A drop of water fell on the toe and I began rubbing it into the leather with my rag.

Another drop fell behind that one. I quickly tried to erase the tear by rubbing it into the surface of the oxford in my hand. I began buffing and brushing like a madman, oblivious to anyone else in the room. I determined not to stop until I saw my face in my father's shoes. They were shining, but not enough to show my gratitude to the man who taught me all I know about being a man.

Then it occurred to me, that I shouldn't be looking for my face in my father's shoes, but instead looking for my face in my father's footsteps.

When I looked at how he loved his wife, do I see that love reflected in my relationship?

When I glance over the scope of his ministry and how his life's work was to lift others up, do I see his reflection in my own life?

I looked down at the shoe...it looked back up at me. I held it up across the room for Dad to see. He nodded his approval.

I got started on the next pair and Romans 10:15 came to mind, "How beautiful are the feet of them that preach the gospel of peace, and bring glad tidings of good things."

17

Talking To God

Young Raphael, handsome, athletic, smart. He fell in love with his college sweetheart. They got married. He told her he would provide everything she wanted.

He loved God. He went to church.

Life began to happen. Illness struck his young bride. He worked several jobs. There were times when he would wake up before dawn and go to work at the radio station. After he hung up the headphones from that job, it was off to the next assignment, substitute teacher at a local school. When the bell rang, it was time for his main job at the television station. He did what he had to for his family.

He prayed.

Later the couple had children. One child was diagnosed with autism.

He prayed.

An aunt who was more like a sister to him was diagnosed with cancer. He prayed like there was no tomorrow. The aunt died. That hurt.

The autism diagnosis became a severe strain on his family. He prayed.

His father, his rock, his pastor, and his friend was diagnosed with dementia. He said, God, what's up? He prayed fervently. He fasted. His father's condition worsened. His father had spent most of his life serving God and God's people. What kind of retirement plan is this?

He watched his father decline, he watched his son's mental health spiral. God. What's up? He watched his family, struggle with mental illness. His wife, his children driven to tears? Hey, God are you watching this? Any day now would be cool. Fix this- please, in Jesus' name amen.

His father eventually became bedridden.

He tried to talk to him. But found it extremely difficult to do. Sometimes he was there physically, but not mentally. The son would talk, but he wasn't really sure that the father could hear him.

He felt like he was wearing a heavy-weighted vest. He was wrapped up in a depression so heavy that it began to be uncomfortably, comfortable.

Fine God, if you're not going to talk to me, then I'm not going to talk to you. And I pulled the covers up over my head.

But He wouldn't let it go. Thankfully.

"What are you doing?" He asked.

"I'm ignoring You like You ignore me."

"I deserve that?" He questioned.

"What do you mean? " I asked.

"After all that we've done together, you're turning away from me because a few things didn't go your way?"

"You told me I could move mountains," I retorted. "You told me I only needed a grain of a mustard seed-sized faith. You led me to believe that no request was too hard for you. And when I need you most, it's like you aren't taking my calls or something."

"I see," He said. "Have I ever shown up for you?"

"Sure. You healed my wife. You healed my oldest daughter, Jaydn. You helped me get a new job that paid better. You put me in situations that allowed me to use my gifts. You've done a lot for me, but you have also been silent when I've asked for help on behalf of the people closest to me."

"I see", He said.

"I see?", I asked incredulously. 'I see?' That's all you've got for me?"

No answer. He was gone. The conversation was over.

18

Hymning and Hawing

"I need thee, oh I need thee. Every hour I need thee."

Those are the words of a church hymn I grew up singing. But I don't like feeling needy. If it were up to me I would go through life helping and being helpful to others, but handle my own business, on my own. I don't like other people being in my business.

Just me and God.

If I have a problem I can't handle, I hand it over to God, and he promptly takes care of it. Right? Isn't that how it's supposed to be? I shouldn't have to burden others with my problems.

God you said, "Cast your cares on me." You didn't say cast them on my neighbor. I desire a personal savior. But I keep being redirected to your representatives.

I believe in your power and ability. Isn't that enough? What I'm asking of you isn't that hard for you to do, considering your resume. But here I sit. Still waiting. How long must I wait? I feel like I've been patient. I feel like you could have responded by now.

I've given you opportunities to handle it. I've sat back waiting to behold the deliverance of the Lord. I have cried and begged for your help, but it feels like I am being mocked in the face of my troubles.

So what do I do when you don't answer? I guess I am forced to seek the inferior help of man.

Why must I waste valuable time with an intern when the master healer himself says he will never leave me or forsake me?

I went into this, excited at the prospect of receiving this miracle from you. I didn't realize I'd have to work so hard for it. Yes, faith is work. Continuing to believe when all signs show it's probably not going to happen, is work.

And you know what? Maybe you saying, 'I hear you but just a bit longer' would be nice. Even the lying doctors and nurses care enough to say that. Acknowledge that I'm here and that my request has been heard and is being honored in the order that it was received. Something.

You are my secret weapon against any problem. If my best weapon doesn't work where does that leave me?

> "I need thee oh I need thee.
> Every hour I need thee.
> Oh, bless me now my savior.
> I come to thee."

My father is missing, mentally. I go to my heavenly Father for help with that, and can't seem to find Him either. Whither shall I turn for help now?

> "Father, I stretch my hands to thee.
> No other help I know.
> If thou withdraw thyself from me,
> tell me whither shall I go?"

Hymns of comfort...or just strong spiritual memories?

This is all I've got, God. While I'm over here "hymning" you seem to be hawing. When will you hear my cry? When will you deliver me?

19

SUMMONED

I sat in the waiting area anxiously, not knowing what to expect. I had been summoned to His office and I had no idea what kind of mood He was in, or why I had been called.

The receptionist came up to me with a slight smile and said, "The Lord will see you now. Right this way."

When I entered the office He was sitting in a high-backed chair with his back towards me. His voice thundered, "I heard you've had some complaints about me and the way that I do things around here."

I froze in my seat terrified. His chair slowly swiveled around toward me. Two thunderbolts were in his left hand and he twirled them between his fingers.

I stuttered, "Good day, Your Majesty, Your Excellency, wonderful is your name, and blessed ab-", He cut me off mid-sentence.

"Save it." He snapped his fingers and when he did, my manuscript appeared where the lightning bolts had been. He shuffled through the pages and looked at me. "This how you feel about me?"

I thought, 'this is where I should apologize profusely and beg for His forgiveness,' but I knew it was too late. Barely above a whisper I managed, "At the time I did, Lord."

"And now?" He asked.

I lowered my head and nodded. "Yes, my Lord."

"I see," He replied

"You said that the last time, too" I reminded Him.

"I know."

"May I speak freely, my Lord?" I mumbled meekly.

"Oh, " he said with some amusement, "Now you want to ask? Sure. Go ahead."

"My Lord, you have allowed some people close to me to suffer greatly. In turn, the rest of us have endured immense pain. Despite our pleas, it seems in our hour of need you…turned a deaf ear towards us," I finished.

"Is that what you think?" he inquired.

I nodded.

"I see. That suit that you're wearing now. Did you wear that yesterday?"

"No, my Lord. Yesterday I wore a different outfit."

"And when you disrobed, did you mourn for that outfit? Did you cry and grieve for it, when you took it off?"

Puzzled, I tilted my head and answered, "No. Why would I?"

He motioned to a closet in the corner of the room. "There would be no need to mourn that set of clothing would it, because it's right here with you. The "clothes" didn't go anywhere, did they? Plus, you have countless other vestiture to choose from. Correct?"

I nodded.

"Come with me," he said. Once at the closet, He motioned me inside.

What I saw startled me. "God," I stammered, "this is MY closet."

"Yes, that's right. Your closet with all of your different clothing. Suits and shirts for more formal occasions, sweats for exercising, more casual relaxing get-ups and accessories. But there is one important thing I want you to notice; and it's a good thing for you, too. Have you noticed that your clothing doesn't talk back to you?"

I am super perplexed by now. "I don't understand."

"Would you like to hear them? Your clothes?" He clapped his hands and I had to cover my ears from the discordant noises that came from my wardrobe. It was as if every garment I owned was having a debate.

My suits: "He wears us every time he goes somewhere special. I know that we're his favorite.

An Old shirt: "He hasn't worn me in forever. I don't know why. I keep hoping that he will pick me again, but he seldom does. I must not be important to him anymore.

Running shoes: "Well he uses me all the time but he doesn't appreciate me. Every time he slams my face into the ground. When he's not careful to watch his step I get covered in poo. Nobody has it worse than me.

Yard shoes: "Are you kidding me. I've got manure embedded in places I don't even know about. You think I'd get a proper wash every now and again right? But no. He doesn't appreciate that I keep him safe from thorns and thistles. He just takes me off and tosses me in the back of the closet. Some life that is."

"This is dreadful, Lord will you make it stop?" I beg of Him.

With a wave of his hand, the room is quiet again. "That was a very 'ear-opening' moment for you wasn't it?"

"That's how my clothes feel about me?" I asked sheepishly. "I didn't know."

"How could you have known? Now that you know, what will you do differently?"

I thought for a moment. "Well, honestly Lord, nothing. These are MY clothes. They are for my benefit, not me for theirs. Each of them is in my wardrobe for different purposes, reasons, and seasons. I'm not going to let my clothes dictate what I do with my life and when I do it..."

As soon as I heard the words come out of my mouth, I saw a broad grin break across God's face. "You set me up," I said.

He laughed a great big hearty laugh, "Got 'eem!"

I had to laugh. "Yes. You got me."

"Raphael, listen," he said to me as he rested an arm on my shoulder, "I am not a man, I am spirit. I don't have a body. I gifted the earth to mankind. When I see work on the earth that needs to be done. I prepare a body, fill it with my spirit, and say 'Go.'"

"But God, what about the whole free will thing?" I asked.

"What about it? You ALL have free will. You can pick and choose what you will or will not do. But each mission has specific instructions and before you come back to me, My will WILL be done. Like you, I have many different types of bodies/outfits for a variety of different missions. If you choose to live a life that compromises your longevity, I won't stop you. If you choose to live a life against the rules that I have strongly suggested you follow, you are choosing to live in discomfort, and that's on you. But you will perform the mission that I sent you to perform. That is non-negotiable."

"So it is impossible for you to mourn like we mourn or be sensitive to our prayers?"

"No. Not impossible. I know you hurt, but you can't see the full picture like I can. And that my dear boy, is why you have to Trust me, or not."

"Does it bother you when we don't trust you?"

"Not at all. That's really your problem. Whether you believe in me or not, I'm still here. Whether you trust in me or not, I'm still here and you're still always going to carry out MY will. The TRUST isn't for me at all, TRUST in me is designed for you. TRUST is crafted through LOVE. When you TRUST me you don't have to continue living in FEAR. Fear is what makes living hard for you."

Lying on a hangar in the office is a white garment. He hands it to me. "Look at the label. Read what it says."

I reply, "It says PEACE."

"What's it made out of?" he yells back.

"LOVE."

"Try it on."

I close the door to the closet and pull on the robe. "It feels like a warm hug!" I shout back excitedly, "and it smells heavenly!"

"Yep," He answers looking at me with a quizzical gaze as I emerge from behind the door.

"What's wrong? What did I do?" I asked confused by His expression.

He smiled back and asked, "Why did you close the door when you changed into the robe?"

Before I could think I answered, "Because I was getting dressed and I didn't want you to see me naked."

Satisfied at my answer he smirked and said, "I see."

"What do you see? Please tell me."

"I see that you were willing to accept my PEACE, but you were still unwilling to show me your vulnerability. My son, I see your heart. I know ALL of your struggles. But until you can learn to relax in my Love for you, you'll never fully enjoy my PEACE."

I looked down to find myself back in my old clothes. I hung my head.

"But I am broken."

"No, you're not."

"I'm not enough."

"Not without me."

"You don't move soon enough when I call you."

"I've already solved your problem before you call."

"I'm afraid that you won't come through for me."

"You are choosing to wear a garment of fear. It's fabric cannot compare to Love. Choose LOVE. Choose Peace. TRUST. Not for my sake, my son, but for yours."

20

A Thousand Steps In the Dark

One part of the reason these memories are so hard to discuss is that I have shoved them so far back into my cranial storage spaces that the details are a bit hazy. They aren't packed so far away that I can't reach them, but they were put away with such anger and hurt that they may be damaged.

(I can jump right into my emotions of having to be in the hospital, but the build up is so painful. He's been there several times. Trying to remember the circumstances of what caused him to go there each time...I've blocked it out.)

In my lifetime, I've been blessed to know men and women who could hear from God. In my faith, we refer to them as prophets. They share with you something about your life that they have seen in the spirit realm. Then you have three options: you can accept it, you can reject it, or you can take the attitude "we'll see". I tend to lean towards "we'll see." If what you've told me is true then after we put some time on it, we will see.

One such gentleman had been spot on for years. He would share some things with me and every single time, those things would come to pass. Through this pattern, I developed a sense of trust in his prophecies.

But one day as I was discussing my son and pouring out my heart to him about my concerns and fears, he gave me advice that really made me scratch my head.

Grant was getting older and bigger, and as such, emotional outbursts were growing more outrageous as well. I feared that he would act out in the presence of someone who didn't know him and things wouldn't end well. That law enforcement would have to get involved.

I have reported on so many cases of unarmed black men dying at the hands of police. What could I do to keep my son safe? How could I keep him from escalating into rage in the first place?

This minister suggested that maybe I shouldn't fear law enforcement interference. Maybe I should let the law get involved so that my son could see and feel the consequences of his behavior. He suggested that I might be hindering God's plan to help my son, by trying to keep him out of trouble.

This I rejected. There's no way this is what God would want. The police are killing black people out here. No way. You've been right about so many other things, but you've finally missed God on this one, I thought.

Not very long after that conversation, Grant had a meltdown that wouldn't let up. He raised his hand at his mother and I went crazy. We tussled out in the garage. My goal was to restrain him until he was able to calm down. He never calmed down. After an hour of pinning him (so that he wasn't a danger to himself or me) I concluded that I couldn't do this forever. I told Sarena that she'd have to call the police. If he wasn't calming down after all this time, there was no way he was going to be able to stay there with us.

Sarena dialed 9-1-1 and explained the situation to dispatch. She was very careful to let them know that our son was on the autism spectrum and that he was having an episode. The last thing she wanted was for things to get even further out of hand.

The first responding officer showed up in a way that set the tone for the rest of the encounter. He calmly approached us all and began asking Grant questions. His approach was even-keeled. He later explained to us that he had a relative on the autism spectrum. Moments later, a similar exchange when his supervisor arrived. She too, had a family member on the spectrum and they approached our situation delicately.

I let Sarena do most of the talking. By this time, I was worn out physically and drained emotionally. I was hurt that things had to get to this point and I was embarrassed. But I also wanted my son to get the help that he needed. This part was all new to us and we didn't really know what to expect next.

Grant was now much calmer than he had been before. They offered to take him down to the Children's hospital and we obliged with the hope that maybe someone there could give him the help that he needed. We had been trying unsuccessfully to get him in to be seen by one of the most highly recommended doctors who specialized in autism. Hopefully, this ugly episode would put us closer to Grant getting the care that he needed.

Once he arrived at the emergency room, he began to make friends with all of the doctors and nurses there. He is an outgoing guy, he does have some difficulty with social cues at times (the reason why we were here), but his favorite thing is meeting new people. All of that would soon nearly backfire on us.

When I got to the hospital, I was told that a psychiatrist would visit with Grant. He had gotten some sort of tranquilizer by this time, I suppose for everyone's safety.

I was told that they would be discharging Grant. There was nothing more they could do. There were no beds available at the Institute of Psychiatry and they didn't really feel that was the best place for him.

We were crushed. I calculated that in a few hours when the shot they had given him wore off and he began to remember what had set him off in the first place, the cycle was going to start all over again and what would we have to show for it? More dents in the furniture and holes in the wall.

I demanded that they do more. I took down their names and told them that if any member of our family were injured as a result of a future outburst later in the evening that I would hold each of them accountable. What was happening in Grant's mind was beyond our control. I was hopeful that someone at that huge medical facility could sit him down, and talk to him. Get to the bottom of what was making him act that way. I was hopeful that someone could explain to us why some thoughts got stuck in his brain and made him rage out!

But that didn't happen. As soon as they deemed him "not a threat to himself" they told us to take him home. There was no place for him to go. The beds at the mental facilities were all full. "Your son has autism, deal with it. It's not going to get better", we were told.

After a few times of going through that revolving door, we began to feel that the help we were expecting for our son, didn't exist. The people we thought could help us, said there was very little they could do.

Eventually, a bed opened up at the Institute of Psychiatry and they admitted Grant. While he was in the children's ER I could come by and visit him after my shift. But when he was moved to the psychiatry ward there were strict visiting hours.

These were rough days for our family. It was not easy at home to pass Grant's room and know that he wasn't there. However, we were hopeful that finally, he would get the attention and the care that he needed from people who knew what they were doing.

Even though I couldn't get in to see him, I remember going down to the hospital and just staring at the building. I prayed. I cried. I prayed and cried, and then I walked. I encircled that building and I called on God.

The cadence of my footsteps matched the rhythm of my prayers as I made my way around the campus. "God please heal my son. Please bless the nurses and orderlies assigned to his floor. Keep your angels of protection around them all. Touch the other patients, Father. Heal their minds. Give them comfort. Allow them to find the help that they were sent here to receive. Keep an angel around Grant. Don't allow any negative spirits to attach to him while he is in this place. Keep your angels close, God", I prayed.

I did several prayer laps around that facility. If the earnestness of my plea was the cost of healing, everyone in that building would have been discharged THAT night. But even though I had prayed myself sleepy, and worn a path around the campus there was little confirmation that my verbal assault on heaven had made any impact.

Nine hundred twenty-six steps. I went back and retraced them months later. Each lap around was nearly a thousand steps. In the bible, the children of Israel marched around the walls of Jericho seven times, and on the seventh lap they were victorious. God, I'm out here. If it takes seven laps, please just say the word. We've been walking this out physically, spiritually, and psychologically for more than a dozen years. It's got to get better than this.

What do we have to do for you to bring down the walls of rage and anger, consuming thoughts and troubling behaviors?

After several hours, I realized I had done all that I could do. If nothing else I felt a little lighter, less fearful, and more hopeful. So I went home.

Another time when he had to stay overnight, I was called down to the unit. They told me he was having a difficult time. Whatever thought that was stuck in his head would not let him go. He was wrestling with it and was inconsolable.

The security guards stood post at the doors keeping a watchful eye. I approached my son with a firm voice and tone. I reached my hands out to him palms up and asked, "Can I help you?"

"Yes," he answered, calming down a bit but still very heightened by the situation. He took hold of my hands and we stood toe to toe facing each other in the hallway.

This technique of holding hands I stumbled upon through much trial and error. Mostly error. In retrospect, if I had known how to deploy this de-escalation tactic earlier, he may not have had to come down here the very first time.

Months earlier he had become inconsolable at the house. Nothing we said or did would allow the rage to pass. I took him out to the empty garage where he was less likely to damage our home or anyone in it. He kicked, he screamed, he cursed, he threw things and then I felt I had to do something quickly. So I did what I thought I had to do. I grabbed him in a bear hug and held him on the floor waiting on him to get tired and settle down.

It didn't happen. For 45 minutes I wrestled on the floor with him trying to keep him from harm. Until finally I told Sarena we needed to call the police.

I handled it all wrong. I would later find out that he took my putting him in a bear hug as a sign of aggression. He interpreted my actions as hostile and in his mind he had to fight back to get free. It pains me now to realize this. In fact, I had an opportunity to speak to a group of young people involved in an autism program at the medical university and they confirmed to me in no uncertain terms that they do not like unsolicited touching. For some of them it felt uncomfortable. To others, it was taken as a sign of disrespect.

Now, I extend my hands to him, palms up, and wait. I present myself to him to let him know, "Hey I'm not going to grab you. I'm not here to hurt you I only want to help. Since I have been doing this, there has NEVER been a situation where I have approached him in this manner and he has not calmed down to the point where he could meet me at least holding hands together.

When HE grabs hold of my hand I squeeze it lightly and say, "Who am I?"

"You're my Dad", he'll say sometimes through tears.

"Am I here to hurt you?", I ask.

"No."

"Do I love you?"

"Yes."

"OK. What's wrong?"

It's a beautiful thing to watch the tension leave his shoulders ever so slightly as he begins to explain what's bothering him in more manageable tones. I let him talk. I ask questions to make sure I understand. I ask questions and make him confirm that he intends to convey what I am hearing him say.

Generally, at that point, we can have a conversation. He feels heard. The situation that got him worked up in the first place has not changed, but he is free to let go of some of the anxiety that accompanied him to such an unpleasant place.

This is what we did in the hallway of the Psych ward with security personnel looking on. They eventually relaxed their posture as Grant and I both took seats on the floor outside of his room.

I could not change his situation. He wanted to go home. But I tried my best to replace the thoughts that were giving him anxiety with more pleasant scenarios. We played "I spy" in the hallway. I told him to tell me a memory from his favorite day at the beach.

After a while he was okay. He had some things to look forward to. I hugged him and told him I loved him while he went back to his room. As I was leaving, one of the security guards approached me and said that what he had just watched was one of the most tender things he'd ever seen. I remember thanking him for sharing that, but I couldn't help thinking to myself, why isn't it enough to keep him out of here?

21

"Out of Control"

It was not a big deal when my son decided to walk/hike to the top of a grassy hill in downtown Greenville, South Carolina. We were exploring the Falls at Reedy Creek and enjoying ourselves.

With his headphones on his ears and standing at the top of the hill (about a 50-foot elevation), he appeared to be the king of the mountain. Then he got the idea that he would run down the hill. It took no time for him to realize that his descent was happening at a far faster rate than his climb. With every step, his speed doubled. His wide-open eyes were filled with fear as he began to realize that he was out of control.

Standing at the bottom of the hill, I braced for impact. I think I was hoping that he would find a way to stop, or at least slow his run. He did not. Instinctively, I broadened my stance, hunkered down, opened my arms, and prepared for the impending collision.

Twenty feet away...10 feet away...5 feet...I reached out to him, he threw out his arms towards me and BOOOM, leaped into my arms!! My lip went into his chest, my neck snapped back. My ankle (my already weak ankle) protested under the weight and nearly gave way, but it did not let me fall. I did not let my son fall.

I imagine that's what it feels like to be hit by an NFL lineman at full speed.

Once we all caught our breath and realized just how blessed we had been in that moment, another thought sat down beside me on the stone wall.

I have tried to be there for my son in every way since the day that he was born. I am fiercely protective of my family. I vowed to do anything in my power to keep them safe. Had he been smaller, this whole thing, wouldn't have been a thing. I would have snatched him up, spun him around, and sent him off to play some more. But this was different. It took everything in me to catch him and protect him this time. He's older and stronger now. I'm older and maybe not as strong as I used to be. What happens when I'm no longer enough to catch him when he's out of control?

For some time now, my wife and I have been working on teaching Grant to control himself. We are trying to show him the importance of being in control of his thoughts, his feelings, his emotions, and his rage. God has gifted me a portion of patience during this difficult time in our lives.

Whereas a few years ago, I would react explosively, towards my son, there is now a measure of grace and long-suffering. I have attempted to embody the biblical admonition that a soft answer turneth away wrath. I have seen amazing results and awe-inspiring conversations between my son and me during this process.

But even with all of that, a nagging question resides rent-free in the dark corners of my mind, "What happens if one day you can't reach him? What happens when none of your strategies work anymore? What happens when love alone is not enough?

It is a scary thought. And if I dwell on it too long, fear begins to move in. That fear paints a mural on the walls of my mind that looks eerily similar to the look in Grant's eyes, as he ran down that hill.

But the bible tells us in **Psalm 91** that he who dwells in the shelter of the most high shall abide under the shadow of the Almighty.

4 He shall cover thee with his feathers, and under his wings shalt thou trust: his truth shall be thy shield and buckler.

When those gathered at the park that day saw my son out of control, they saw that fear in his face. They saw gravity hastening his steps toward rocks and rails and destruction. They saw a man standing at the bottom of the hill bracing for only God knows what. They saw strangers' jaws drop as the collision occurred. But what they didn't see was God standing behind me, with his arms open wide catching BOTH of us.

9 Because thou hast made the Lord, which is my refuge, even the most High, thy habitation;

10 There shall no evil befall thee, neither shall any plague come nigh thy dwelling.

11 For he shall give his angels charge over thee, to keep thee in all thy ways.

12 They shall bear thee up in their hands, lest thou dash thy foot against a stone.

14 Because he hath set his love upon me, therefore will I deliver him: I will set him on high, because he hath known my name.

15 He shall call upon me, and I will answer him: I will be with him in trouble; I will deliver him, and honour him.

16 With long life will I satisfy him, and shew him my salvation.

It all could have ended so badly. However, because I was in a position to catch my son and absorb the blow, God was able to keep us both before we were dashed to pieces on the banks of those falls.

This event has encouraged me to continue to be in the right position. It doesn't matter what it looks like. If I do what I'm supposed to do, if I'm true to where He has put me, He is there to handle the rest, I don't have to do it all on my own. I can't do it all on my own. But if I do my part, it will all work out. I can't fall apart because my child is out of control. I can't be out of position or angry when he's in crisis.

He could not physically stop the momentum of his fall. And I realize now that there are times when he can not physically stop himself once rage has set in.

He has learned from this experience that running down hills is not wise because you can lose control of your actions. Hopefully, we can apply that lesson to his emotional states and teach him that it's a lot easier to stop the swift plummet into emotional distress when you don't let your emotions rise that high.

Don't give up parents. Don't give up caregivers. You are not in this alone. God will not leave you alone or comfortless. There is value in what you are doing. Even when it looks like no one notices or appreciates the work that you do. You are in position. You are right where you are supposed to be. Stay there. Stand still. Don't move. And brace yourself for salvation.

22

"It's Morning"

A t five minutes of 6 this morning, there was a knock on my bedroom door. On the other side of it, my little boy, Grant. I wipe
the sleep from my eyes and look up to his hulking frame filling the
doorway and he asks, "Can we go on a 'gratitude walk'?"

We've taken "Gratitude Walks" before. It was an idea I came up
with once when he was having difficulty coping with relentless, troubling thoughts. That time we went on a tour of our neighborhood
and alternated sharing things for which we were grateful. It brought

him to a happier space then. So when he suggested that we go on one I said, "Let me grab my shoes."

The Champ had a rough day yesterday. He had barely been at school half an hour and they were already calling for us to come and get him. What could have gone wrong already?!

It turns out that someone had declined his invitation for a hug. Which is fine. People have boundaries and we are learning to respect those boundaries. But we are also struggling to learn the difference between rejection and a person's right to autonomy. Things didn't go well. He spent the day having to re-evaluate his actions.

Then the morning came with a knock on my door and an invitation to walk. So walk we did. As we started our trek I said, "What are you grateful for?"

He said, "I'm thankful for fist bumps."

Fist bumps. YES! I'm thankful for fist bumps, too. My son was growing up in front of my eyes. I suppose sometime through the night as he reflected on the previous day, it dawned on him that in lieu of a hug from his friend a fist bump would have sufficed!

It may not seem like much to you, but this was huge. It appeared that he got the message that we were trying to teach in his own time. He was starting this day with much clearer head space and HE initiated these efforts.

Our walk continued and he proceeded to run off dozens of other things that he was grateful for. I told him I was proud of him and allowed him to listen to music on his headphones for the rest of the walk if he wanted to. Then it was my turn to be grateful. Thank you, God for the kids that you've given us. Thank you for this giant of a kid who really is trying every day to be a better man. Help me to be enough for him.

I turn around and see him smiling a broad smile and singing along with the music in his headphones,

"I am responsible I am responsible
I get better every single day

I get better every single day
I'm surrounded by love..."

My wife and I have had to constantly talk to Grant about the kind of music that he's listening to. But this morning he was listening to Snoop Dogg's "Affirmation Song" full of positive and motivating messages. Another sign that he was determined to have a great day. I love this kid!

Years ago, when I worked part-time as a substitute teacher I discovered that the students were more productive if I let them listen to music. It was a music list that I carefully cultivated of tunes that were positive, light, and motivating but still something that the kids would be interested in hearing.

As I was making the mix tapes I thought, "Wouldn't it be great if every artist that our kids listen to, committed to putting at least ONE positive track on each album!" I said if I ever got an audience with the Snoop Dogg's and the Ice Cube's and other artists, I would challenge them to do so.

This song by Snoop went hard this morning on our gratitude walk. It is one that I will put in heavy rotation on my personal playlist.

"Every problem has an answer
Every problem has an answer
I deserve to feel good
I deserve to feel good
Anything is possible
Anything is possible
I believe in myself
I believe in myself
I can control my own happiness
I can control my own happiness.

This morning I realized, that I am wealthy in the things that matter. Rich moments like this one, walking around the neighborhood with my son blasting music by Snoop Dogg. I am grateful for affirmations. I am grateful for second chances and new songs. I am grateful for the morning because that's when the joy comes.

"The 'Whatsoever Things'"

*P*hilippians 4:8
Finally brethren, whatsoever things are true, whatsoever things are honest, whatsoever things are just, whatsoever things are lovely, whatsoever things are pure, whatsoever things are of good report, if there be any virtue, if there be any praise, think on these things.

Grant had had a string of successful days. Days where he was in full and complete control. He wears his diagnostic light in his face. When his eyes are bright, and cheeks are high, that smile dazzles any room. When you see that sign, the Champ is in his zone. He is inquisitive. He throws himself into his research on important topics like where he wants to go to college and where he plans to have his birthday party. When he is locked in, he is the life of the party. His essence is joy. He dances to a rhythm that he alone can hear and smiles as the world watches him.

But then there are days when the system crashes and his diagnostic display across his face becomes clouded. The smile is replaced by frustration, or worse anger. The laughter gives way to shouts and outbursts. You can almost count the seconds before his gaze erupts into a full meltdown.

It's never anything major, to us. His inability to recall a person's name. His ability to recall that when he spoke to the cashier on Wednesday, she didn't ask how HE was doing. When he gets into this mode, a parade of similar thoughts overwhelms his brain space until he can't take it anymore.

When we notice the storm brewing I approach him and try my best to reason with him. I try to explain that this is a moment for self-control. This is the time to dismiss these little thoughts before they grow into great big monsters and cause him to do things that he will regret.

He may be able to put off the intrusive thoughts for a while, but usually, the train has already left the station and in a few moments will have picked up a dozen more thoughts equally detrimental to his mental state.

If it persists, usually I have to escalate things with physical exertion. We workout. Jumping jacks, flutter kicks, planks, wall sits, push-ups. Set after set after set. He screams and grunts and pushes his way through. I don't know exactly what it is, but midway through the workout, the thoughts that once troubled him are gone. Maybe they drowned in the pool of sweat that has now formed on the garage floor. But I can see that the Champ is coming back.

That doesn't mean we stop though. I hug him, give him a fist bump, and tell him I'm glad he's back, but we've got two more sets to go. After a quick water break its back to the grind.

He's tired. I see it. He is in a better place. I know it. But we've still got further to go.

Now, I get to coach him. I get to pour into him. I get to yell, "You can do this CHAMP!!"

Let's go, you've got this. DON'T YOU DARE LET YOUR FEET TOUCH THE FLOOR!"

He loves the encouragement. He digs deeper. If he ever thought this was punishment, when I begin to motivate him he realizes the shift in atmosphere and responds. Now, its about personal best. It's about not giving up. It's about following through. It's about being accountable. His eyes tell me that as tough as this is, he doesn't want to let me down. My eyes say you are my son, as long as you don't quit you won't let me down.

After that, we can talk. He can see more clearly what led up to his lapse in self-control. He understands a little better how he can deal with it in the future, but he's proud of himself for making it to the other side.

"I'm HAPPY NOW!!!" he exclaims to the world.

But the other day, we didn't make it to the workout round. It wasn't necessary.

The petty nagging thoughts of the day would not leave him alone. He sat up in his bed and screamed. I led him downstairs, but instead of the workout that I had promised him I led him to Philippians 4:8 and made him read it over and over again.

Then we had a conversation about the "Whatsoever things".

There are six whatsoever things...true, honest, just, lovely, pure, of good report.

I made him highlight those six whatsoever things. Then I asked him to examine his thoughts. The thought that made you scream at the top of your lungs was it true, honest, just, lovely, pure or of good report?

No.

The thoughts you had earlier were they true, honest, just, lovely, pure or of a good report?

He said no.

So if they aren't give me some thoughts that are.

He rattled off his college choices, his birthday party, going on vacations and on and on and on. That's all it took. The smile was back.

What does the rest of the scripture say?

If there be any virtue, if there be any praise, think on these things.

Those are the kinds of things you need to focus your mind on son. Not who said what to you at school three days ago. Don't give your time to thoughts that you know are not going to build you up.

I made him memorize that verse. We broke it down and when we put a little beat to it, oh he was a whole new dude! He went through the house screaming, "if there be any virtue, if there be any praise, THINK ON THESE THINGS!"

For emphasis when he gets to the end of the scripture I told him to touch his head four times as he said THINK ON THESE THINGS!

He loved it. That worked...today. I am hopeful that when he has another crisis of thoughts (and he will) that he will think back to that scripture and perhaps, shift his mindset.

That verse is one of my mother's favorite verses. She often recited it to me when the distractions of life seemed to be overwhelming. It sounded so heavenly and righteous when I read it, and so not for me. I wasn't in the mood for bumble bees, flowers and classical music. But over time, I came to realize that those were my lovely things.

When I am overwhelmed, sitting alone in a garden, or near the water and listening to a concerto really does have a calming effect. It allows me to reset. After thinking on those things, The thing that I dreaded moments before doesn't seem to hold the same power over me as it did before.

I've come to find that when life throws all kinds of things at me, when my mind won't settle, when my spirit is disturbed, spending some time with my "whatsoever things" allows me to take the focus off of my troubles and magnify my God.

23

My Son's First Sermon

For all of the challenges that my son Grant deals with self confidence is not one of them. If he sees anyone in the family accomplish a thing he just assumes that he is capable of the same. I like that about him. A few weeks ago his younger sister, Nia was called upon to give the mini message on youth Sunday. She did a wonderful job and we were all so proud of her.

Later that day he went up to his aunt, the youth leader, and asked when it would be his turn to bring the youth message. His aunt smiled and said, well I guess we'll hear from you next youth Sunday. That was all he needed to hear.

He began to prepare his sermon as if he had done it a million times. He typed up his presentation. I work in the media ministry at our church and the night before his big sermon he said, "Dad I need you to help me make scripture slides for my message tomorrow."

I was blown away. He knew exactly which scriptures he wanted to use so I got to work. He showed me his message. It was good.

The next day his aunt stood before the congregation and introduced him, "Our inspirational message is going to come from (he asked me to call him by this title) Dr. Grant James."

The church gave him rousing applause as he sauntered up to the stage with swagger and confidence set to ten. I was nervous, but so proud of him.

"Good morning EOP. How is everyone doing today?" he began. "My name is Grant James, I am in my senior year of high school!" His excitement was met with more energy from the pews.

He continued, "When I was younger I couldn't talk. I have had autism since I was two years old. When I was frustrated I yelled a lot. Sometimes it was hard to explain things. I used the chalkboard wall in my kitchen to write and draw. Sometimes I still get frustrated but I am learning to do breathing exercises, go on walks, and read scriptures. One of my favorite scriptures is Philippians 4:8. Everybody please rise on your feet and repeat after me. I'm going to do my moves," he instructed.

In his own voice and cadence, he began to almost sing the verse as the audience echoed back the refrain.

"It says Finally brethren, Whatsoever things are true, Whatsoever things are honest. Whatsoever things are just, whatsoever things are pure, whatsoever things are lovely, whatsoever things are of good report. If there be any virtue, if there be any praise, think on these things! Thank you!"

This audience knew Grant before he was born. He grew up right here in this church. These members have cheered him on every step of the way, and they were right there now listening to every word.

"So, I began to think about good things! Good things like I am smart." The crowd roared back their approval. "Good things like I'm doing good at research." More applause. "Good things like I am graduating high school!" and the crowd goes wild. "Good things like I'm going to a college program or joining the workforce. Good things like, God loves me. When I get anxious, I talk to myself and say calm down. Relax. I also read and I also think about the scriptures.

Psalm 34:4 says, 'I sought the Lord and he heard me and delivered me from all my fears. '

Proverbs 2:6 says, 'For the Lord giveth wisdom out of his mouth cometh knowledge and understanding.'

Proverbs 22:24 says, 'make no friendship with an angry man.'

So hey everybody when you feel frustrated or depressed, put some lavender on because lavender is calming, and think on good things. Thank you, everybody!"

He did it.

He initiated this speaking opportunity. He did the work and he nailed it. I am so proud of this kid. The same child that Sarena and I were told may never speak. This is the same child who we were told may not be able to learn. This is the same child who just got up before a crowd and was vulnerable about his challenges, and he offered encouragement to anyone who had ever felt the same way.

Afterward, so many adults came to me and told me they were blessed by what he shared.

God, I see you. This moment was just, pure, lovely and of good report, (not the doctor's report). Thank you for giving Grant a testimony and thank you for yet another wonderful thing to think on.

24

"Walking and Talking"

Some time ago I discovered that walks around the neighborhood were therapeutic for both me and my son. He looks forward to going on walks and I look forward to joining him and meeting up with him once I get off of work. He absolutely loves taking walks and listening to his music. It offers him a sense of independence and he gets to speak to all the neighbors.

But every now and again while he's making his rounds, a wayward memory of some past hurt (real or imagined) will emerge and he will respond to it emotionally as if it just occurred. Fortunately, we have developed a relationship where he feels comfortable talking to me about these things. In fact, I think he calls me hoping that I can help talk him out of whatever mood he's worked himself into.

When we first started doing this, things were a lot different. He would call me and already be in the middle of a tirade. By this time he would have slung an ungodly amount of curse words into the atmosphere, or maybe kicked over someone's trashcan. Possibly because in one of the encounters with the neighbor they didn't ask him how he was doing after he had inquired about their day.

But he called.

That was the agreement that we had made.

I said to him, "When you feel like you're out of control, call me. Don't just wild out!"

And for the most part that's what he has done. Sometimes I have time to get to him before things escalate further. Sometimes he can hold it together on Facetime long enough for us to talk and walk it out.

I enjoy walking in the cool of the evening. It is refreshing. I too put on my headphones and listen to different lectures or talks on business or some new thing I'm trying to learn. It is very relaxing.

I was about two minutes into my walk today and my phone rang with a Facetime from Grant. Now, it's not always a bad thing to get a call from him while he's out. Sometimes he wants to know where I am in the neighborhood so that we can meet up. But today he needed someone to talk to. I told him I was on my way.

By the time I got to him, I could tell this thing was really burdening him. He would say little things and make gestures that were inappropriate, but they were reflexive emotional reactions to what he was thinking. I didn't scold him for the use of the language, but I did let him know that it was not appropriate and that he needed to stop. I did so with a firm tone, but not a scolding one.

I could see that he was trying to comply so I said, "I know you're upset, but there's a right way to talk about it. Are you going to talk to me like a man or a toddler? Don't whine. Talk."

I set the tone and he changed his tone. In a calm voice, he explained to me what was bothering him. I repeated it back to him so he would know that I understood.

It turns out he had turned to a trusted adult at school when he was having difficulty with something that a classmate said. This is something that we have been working with him on. "When you feel yourself getting out of control, tell an adult."

That was a win. He heard us. He listened to us.

The problem was the adult didn't know how to respond to his statement. I have no doubt they saw that he was emotional and desperately wanted to avoid a meltdown, but were unable to offer what he desired because he didn't have the appropriate language to formulate his request.

For whatever reason, it makes him upset when younger students respond to him by saying, "no sir." We've not really been able to figure it out. But it makes him uncomfortable. He takes it as disrespect.

He was trying to convey that to the adult at school. But she really didn't know what to say.

"So Champ," I began, "you wanted her to give you some advice about how to calm you down because a certain student said 'no sir'?"

"Yes," he said seemingly relieved.

"Ok. That's awesome," I continued. "Trust me she wants to help, but you have to ask her a better question. Without screaming or whining you have to say 'Hey Ms. So-and-So it really bothers me when the kids call me 'sir'. Do you have any advice that could help keep me from getting so upset about that?'"

I asked him if the other student was a friend. He said she was. I said was she being mean to you? He said she was not. I asked him if she was nice. He began to smile and said that she was.

"Well if she's nice and she wasn't mean let's not get upset with her for calling you, sir. It's just a term. She didn't say it as a way to disrespect you. Do you understand?", I asked.

The biggest smile of peace broke out across his face. He did understand that. He immediately dropped the charges in the "emotional wrongdoing" case that he was prosecuting against her in his mind. She was a friend. They were cool. She meant no ill will. All was still right with the world.

That was enough for him to continue his walk. He needed a little pep talk. He needed someone to help him put his emotional train back on track. He just didn't have the vocabulary to ask for what he really craved "in" the moment. Now (for this situation) he does. I have no doubt that if he crafts his questions better and learns how to ask for the help, he will receive it.

As we continued to walk, I told him, "You know who else can help you when you get like this?"

He said, "Who?"

I said, "You! Just like I broke down the situation and got into a calm place and asked certain questions you can do that with yourself."

The Champ was back. An emotional crisis had been averted. He put on his headphones, I put on my interview and we both continued our walk, his strides more sure and free. A few moments later I heard him ask me, "Dad, do you forgive me for making those gestures and saying those things back there a few minutes ago?"

I stopped cold in my tracks and opened up my arms to him trying to hold back tears. "Come here, of course, I forgive you, son. We all make mistakes. I make mistakes. But what's important is that we learn from them and make them right. You acknowledging your behavior, apologizing for it, and asking for forgiveness was a MAJOR move. Of course, I forgive you. I love you. I've got your back and I'm ALWAYS here for you!"

In that moment as I was talking to my son and feeling pure love and pride for this human being's maturation, I realized that God was speaking directly to me. I heard the voice of God and it sounded eerily similar to my own. I heard God saying (this time to me), "There is nothing that I cannot love you through. There is nothing that you can do or say that would make me withhold forgiveness from my child who is asking for it."

Yes, you showed your butt. Yes, you used inappropriate language. Yes, you were all the way out of pocket, but you apologized and you asked me to forgive you. You are my son! Of course, I will forgive you. More than that, we don't have to talk about it again. You are human, you fell, but you got up again. You addressed your failure and you are working on yourself to keep it from happening again.

The bible called David a man after God's own heart. I never really understood that until this moment. David did a lot of dirt. He killed Goliath and praised God openly, but he did a whole lot of other things that he shouldn't have done.

But now I get it. It's not how bad David sinned, it's his sincerity to make it right.

God don't take your holy spirit away from me.

When I left the house, I (the father) was walking towards Grant's direction just in case he needed me. When he called out to me, I came to him. When he calmly and without fear or frustration laid out his dilemma I was able to help him relax. I was able to provide him a certain measure of peace. We talked. His burden was lifted. He thanked me. He apologized and was concerned that I might not forgive him for his egregious behavior. I told him I would always love and forgive him and I praised him for coming to me and trying to do the right things even when he was uncertain about what to do.

I watched God get a message TO ME, THROUGH ME.

There have been so many struggles that I have undergone in my adult life that have just beat me down time after time again. I've gotten to the point where I stopped praying to God. Why should I? The same thing keeps happening. "This time" I say, "I'm not even going to bother asking you."

So I sit. Angry at God's apparent stubbornness to intervene, I stew.

Then I hear the song I learned in church, *"What a friend we have in Jesus. All our sins and griefs to bear. All because we do not carry, everything to God in prayer."*

I might owe my son an apology.

He handled his situation much better than his Dad. He pleaded with the one who loves him most for help. He made his petition known and was grateful for the encouragement that he was given. He acknowledged his shortcomings and apologized for them and asked for forgiveness.

So now, I'm taking it back to the Lord in prayer. I'm sorry I gave up on you, God. I acted out of character because I didn't think you heard me. I thought you didn't care. But now that you've shown me some things, I see just how much you really do love me. I see that these things weren't done to punish me but to grow me. I see that you love me so much that you were willing to allow me to feel the love that you have for me, through the love that I have for my son.

You have shown me the blessing of falling short. I realize now that if I never failed I would never be able to fully experience the joy of grace. Without the pain of failure, I would never know the feeling of true victory. I now see that without loss it is impossible to feel the bliss that redemption offers. Thank you for this journey. Thank you for being with me (us). I have been wrong. Please accept my apology. I'm better now.

On our walk back home, Grant reached his arms out to me and said, "Dad you're my man! Thank you for always helping me!"

Thank you, son. Thank you, God. For loving me enough, to send me this message that you haven't forsaken me and that you are still with me even when it doesn't feel like it.

"You're my man, God. Thank you for always helping me!"

25

"Eighteenth Birthday'"

J une 20, 2024

Dear Champ,

Congratulations!! In three days you will be 18-years-old, and as you sometimes emphatically exclaim "AN ADULT!"

In the eyes of society and the law at 18 you are considered an adult. That comes with certain privileges, certain responsibilities.

Over the past few days I've watched you trying to "grow" into the number 18. You've tried to order things online, alone. You've taken certain liberties to experience things that you have imagined adults experience.

That's why I'm writing you this letter. I want to give you a blueprint for what I think it will mean for you to officially become a man.

Self-control

Number one is self control. Being a "responsible" adult means being able to control your impulses and desires. At times you will be tempted to ignore the consequences and do whatever you want to do. Resist the urge to do so. Always consider the consequences of your actions. As an adult losing control can cause you to lose everything that you love and value. At all costs, try to remain in control of your emotions, and your temper.

Being an adult is not always fun and glamorous. There are times when it can be very difficult. Find you someone that you trust, someone who will hold you accountable and confide in them. If you feel the need to lose control, find a way to do so in an atmosphere where you don't harm yourself, other people, or property.

This advice is not for you only. There are some people who have been adults for most of their lives who still haven't figured this one out yet.

Character

Son, you are already a man of impeccable character. You have a genuine heart and you care about other people. Don't ever lose that. Preserve your character at all costs. Don't ever get tired of doing the right thing. You will be tempted to act out of character, but don't give in to those urges. When you step outside of who God prepared you to be, life will be very uncomfortable. You are your happiest when you are being "YOU". Speaking to people, helping others, being a friend to your friends, and loving your family puts the brightest smile on your face. That gives you energy. It is a beautiful asset.

Situations will occur that cause you to become angry, frustrated, sad and maybe even depressed but always remember, "God is greater!"

Education

My boy you have a gift when it comes to doing research on the things that interest you. Your determination and resilience are unmatched. Lean into that. Always be willing and hungry to learn new things, attempt new skills. Education does not always equal more schooling. In this present time, there are multiple ways to learn many things for free. Take advantage of them.

Respect

Grant, respect will take you places that money can't get you into. Respecting yourself and others will open doors to unimaginable opportunities. You are more than enough. Don't forget that. If you stay true to that fact, other people will notice your greatness. The first person to show respect to is yourself. You are a pretty dope dude. Don't ever forget it. Respect others. No one is better than you, no one. But you are also no better than them. We are all humans having an earthly existence trying to figure out this thing called life. Always, always, always honor your mother. Without her you would not be here. Never forget that. She has loved you and sacrificed more for you than anyone on the face of the earth. She is to be respected and protected at all costs. Likewise, always respect your sisters. They are special people who love you fiercely. Respect them always.

Finances

Please learn this lesson, my child. Money is just a tool. We use money to obtain the things that we want and need. But you have to be responsible with it. You have to learn to use it in the right ways. If you make a bill, pay it. If you can't afford it, don't get it or find another way to afford it. Be generous with your substance and help others when you can.

God

And finally, maintain a relationship with God. God loves you and wants the best for you. Even when things are not going the way that you planned, trust that God is at work to put you where you need to be.

Champ, being a man is more than just being able to do what you want to do. Sometimes it's about doing what you don't want to do. Getting up early. Going to work. Paying bills. Studying. But you must do what you HAVE to do now so that you can do what you WANT to do later. This is an amazing milestone in your life, but 18 doesn't make you a MAN, your actions do. When you find yourself on the precipice of a stupid decision, take a step back and ask yourself will this decision make me a better man? If the answer is no, then you already know what to do.

The world needs you my boy, but you have to remain in a position of self-control so that when it's time for your gifts and talents to be used you will be able to step up and show everyone why your name is CHAMPION.

I love you, my dude. Have a wonderful 18th birthday.

26

Re: Trust Issues

My Dearest Raphael,

Why do you believe in me? Do you believe in the sun, the moon, the stars? Why? Because you can see them?

Do you believe in the wind? You can't see it? It's direction is only betrayed by the movement of the branches, and the whispers across your face.

The route of the sun has been consistent in your life. You implicitly "trust" that it will rise for you. Do you trust the sun more than its creator?

When you awaken in the morning, you have never once doubted that the floor would be there to greet your feet. You believe that the earth is still there. Do you trust the ground more than the one in heaven?

It seems that your "trust" or "belief" in ME and what I can do is conditional upon whether or not YOU approve of what I am doing. Is that how you feel?

Do you stop believing in the sun when it shines a little too hot for your liking? Do you turn your back on the winter sun and curse it when its rays fail to keep the wind's chill off your back?

Or do you accept that the seasons have changed? You don't just believe in seasonal change, you expect it. You endure each season until its time is up. Do you threaten to withhold your "Trust" from the changing of the seasons? Have you ever said, "I don't believe in you any more spring! My calendar says you should have been here by now but it's still cold!" Or do you simply accept that things aren't going the way you'd like them to go, and move on?

You trust the seasons and their sense of timing, but you question whether you can trust me. I created seasons. You created time. They are not the same.

Not a single leaf would jump back on the tree, because you declared, "There is no autumn." Even though a season may tarry, you trust without question that the next will show up, eventually.

But because I don't answer your prayer in the way you request, you get an attitude. You don't cop that same 'tude with Spring for being too short. I've never heard you pray to me, "Lord, please let the earth have two summer seasons and no winter this year." Why not? You think that's silly? No, you realize that my system is perfect just the way I created it. You realize that each season is necessary, whether you appreciate it or not.

You told me that "Trust" requires a commitment. Does it? How much of a commitment do you have to have to believe in Spring, Summer, Autumn, and Winter?

At the very least, you should try approaching your relationship with me with the same respect you afford my seasons. When summer comes, you don't walk around in a winter coat, refusing to acknowledge the change in seasons. You are more intelligent than that regarding physical concerns. Don't you think it's time to mature concerning spiritual matters?

My spiritual seasons don't always come with forewarnings. They aren't always scheduled on a calendar that you can see. My spiritual seasons, like the physical ones, operate under my instruction.

My advice to you, recognize the season that you are in.

It was a bitter cold season when your father died. But that season won't last forever. Know that another one is on the way. When your spring rolls around, will you be in a position to enjoy it or will you still be sauntering about sulking in your spiritual overcoat?

People enjoy the physical spring—the newness of life, the resurgence of purpose, and the fulfillment of promise. But spring doesn't get a place on the stage until winter completes its performance...spiritually and physically.

Am I worthy of your trust? It doesn't matter. Trust me or not, the world will go on. The seasons will come and go. The sun, moon, and stars will continue their circuits through the heavens. My "WILL", will be accomplished, whether you trust me or not.

Everything I made was perfect. Everything I do benefits you. You may not recognize it right away, or ever, but I make no mistakes.

You, your daughter, and countless others requested a healing that I did not grant. It was not to punish you. Get over yourself. My plan is my plan.

As for the minister who refused to pray for your father's healing, grace is required for him. Though you didn't want to hear it or accept it at the time, his prayer for peace was a most worthy proffer. There is nothing like the warmth of being wrapped, in my peace. It's like a warm spiritual overcoat against the harsh but necessary winds of winter. Pray for the minister. Pray that he experiences the comfort of my peace in his life and for his family.

Your father was one of my finest. He trusted me and knew my voice. But even for Leroy, there was an appointed time for his season to end.

If his season never ended, yours couldn't have begun. You wouldn't have confronted me with these questions. You wouldn't have ever released the feelings that caused you pain. Your spiritual seeds would not have taken root. You would have never written this book. You would have never answered your call to share this message.

I know you don't want to talk about it. I know the process hurts. But I also see what you can't see. I see the many lives your story will touch. I see The ONE person who will be freed up to TALK about it, just because you did. After this, my boy, you will thrive, you will flourish, you will be well-seasoned.

Love without end,

-God

27

My Father's Final Sermon

"There is nothing quite like death, to make us contemplate life."
Those were the first words I uttered to the audience assembled for my father's funeral. At the lectern, my siblings and I each gave our hearts a chance at the microphone. God did not answer my prayers to restore my father's health. He did not reverse the dying process at my behest. So, the heart said what it felt.

"I come to address the elephant in the room. I come to share with you questions that I've asked my God. God, look at all these clouds of witnesses, touch any one of them and they'll tell you 20 things that my father did in service of you, God. It would be one thing to call my father home after serving on the battlefield, but he comes home in his right mind. But God, you saw fit to have him suffer an affliction that caused great pain to our family."

On December 19th, 2022, my youngest brother was there when Dad drew his final breath. The coroner certified the date on the report, but in reality, the father that I knew and loved, died several years earlier when his mental facilities went into decline. He went from being fun and gregarious, to barely there at all.

So on this day, the last day that I would see his face, my heart was in no mood to hold back.

"We loved him through his affliction. We were there with him through the affliction, but the question remained, 'God, why? Why would you do this to someone who lived only for you?'"

"In my feelings, at his bedside, I sat and had an opportunity to talk," I continued. "During those times I found it extremely difficult to talk to Dad. His health had diminished to the point that he was bedridden. At that point, you never knew if you would get a coherent word out of Dad, or if he knew who I was at all. At times it felt a bit silly or awkward to pour out my heart to the man and get no reaction. Over time I stopped expecting a response and satisfied myself with the thought that while he was still on this side, I could share his space and send him feelings of love. Touch his head. Kiss his cheek. Maybe he was aware of it and appreciated it. Maybe he was not.

But on this one particular day, a miracle happened. I sat beside Dad and he was there! Cognizant, alert and smiling. Excitement overcame me, as years of conversations that never happened rushed to the front of my mind, elbowing each other to spend this rare time with Daddy.

At the time, I was having a pretty rough go at things with Grant. So I leaned over and let all of my fears and emotions gush out.

"Dad. you know what I'm going through. Mental illness has affected my family. My wife and I, my girls, my son we have dealt with some pretty sharp shards of mental illness and we don't know why."

I continued, "What do you do when you pray to God and God does not answer your prayer?"

I don't know what I expected him to say. I don't. But I was fully prepared for him to say, "Son look at me...I don't know what you do. I just don't know." That answer would have confirmed my doubts. It would have released me from my expectations of God to come through. It would have made sense had he looked at his own predicament and said, "You know Raphael I thought He would have healed me by now."

But that's not what he said.

"Daddy, what do you do when you pray to God and God does not answer your prayer?"

It was in that moment, that my father would preach his final sermon.

With a feeble voice, but strong conviction, my father looked me right in the face and said, "Trust God."

There was no denying the intent of his words. He said it and he meant it. But still, I pressed further, wondering if he might alter his answer if I presented him with more detailed information.

"But Dad, what if it looks like He doesn't hear you? I fasted. I prayed. I've cried. I've quoted scriptures. I've spoken in tongues, why won't God answer my prayer?"

His reply, though frail, was swift, "Trust God, anyway."

There was conviction in his voice. His words hung on the air between us and His eyes assured me that his answer, was final and he would not take it back.

His final answer was consistent with the life that he lived. The entirety of his journey bore witness to his unwavering trust and belief in God. The songs that he loved to sing, were not merely delightful melodies. They were his mantra.

Every Sunday that man sang! His favorites were "I Won't Complain" by Donnie McClurkin. In my memories, I can see him singing another of his favorites at the top of his lungs,

"I'll rise again, ain't no power on earth can tie me down. Yes, I'll rise again, Death can't keep me in the ground."

Growing up in my church the old saints would sing,

"You can't make me doubt Him, I know too much about him. You can't make me doubt Him, in my heart."

That is who he was. So what was my problem?

Trust God, anyway. I couldn't forget those words. Those words set me on a path. I wanted to be angry at God. I was angry at God. I wanted to give up on everything that I had been taught concerning God, concerning the church. It wasn't working. What was the use in pledging loyalty and devotion to a God, who was going to do what HE wanted to anyway, despite what I begged for, cried for, starved myself for, and quoted scripture for? If He was going to do whatever HE wanted to do, then He could do it without me.

But I kept coming back to those words. Trust God anyway. Every story in the bible in some way boils down to just that. Joseph was sold into slavery, imprisoned, and forgotten. He trusted God through it all. Abraham is in the Faith Hall of Fame because he trusted God. David put his trust in God not his sling, and slew a giant. Job, through all of his trials, trusted God. Jesus, Paul, Peter, John you name it all the way through, the underlying message is no matter what it looks like…trust God.

I glanced out over the Paine College chapel at the sea of clergy, friends, and family and asked, "How many of you are dealing with a loved one who has a mental illness?", several hands went up.

"How many of you have ever questioned God?" even more hands were lifted.

"How many of you have ever wondered? Is God angry at you?", now most people had raised a hand.

"If I take anything away from the sermon that my father lived, it is this," I continued, "we are here and he was called. I imagine a great General in a war room looking out over what's going on in the Earth. His lieutenants are saying, 'We can't communicate with them. They're not answering the communication systems. We have to do something. We have to get them to communicate with us.'

And I hear a voice in the back say, "Send me I'll Go."

"But Leroy, you're gonna have to love these people. They're not doing what they're supposed to do. They're not doing what we sent them to do, but they are very vital to the mission, we have to reclaim them. You can't beat them over the head and bring them back, Leroy. The only weapon that will work is love."

I believe My dad said, "Send me. I'll go. Prepare me a body."

The body was prepared, shot through space, and landed in Florence, South Carolina. There he grew up and got his training. He remembered where he came from, and he remembered his mission and he carried out that mission.

People say my dad was a nice guy, but he was no pushover. He stood firm in his beliefs, and he would debate you about them. He wasn't going to fight you, but he would let you know exactly where he stood. I admire that about my Dad.

My Dad has fought his fight.

"Just like I believe he answered, 'Here am I send me. I'll go' I believe, each of us had that same conversation, for whatever our strength is, for whatever our passion is, for whatever our calling is. That comms system is down. Dad came to help fix it. That comm system is prayer. He brought the people in with love. He showed them how to pray. He showed them how to fix the communication apparatus, that had kept them separated."

"We've got to redefine our mission so that we can fulfill our Godly purpose on this Earth. And in the course of fulfilling that mission if you should ever wonder why, if you should ever wonder, am I doing the right thing? I leave you this from the words of my father on his sick bed suffering from dementia, Trust. God. Anyway. Full stop."

28

Through Sarena's Eyes

Th is book would not have happened without my wife, Sarena. When I couldn't talk about it Sarena encouraged me to get it out. "Just write," she said. "If it's meant to be a book it will minister to you first."

Even when I retreated into myself, she never left me alone. For that, I can never thank you enough. This chapter offers her perspective. She is a brilliant writer who has invited the world to catch brief glimpses into our lives through a blog called onaisle9.com where she advocates for understanding, perspective, and sensitivity toward families with special needs.

Her camera is always ready to capture candid moments. Here are just a few of the moments that captured her heart.

In The Middle

A son standing between his father and his son. Three generations present. Beautiful photo. Beautiful moment. Beautiful blessing. But this was the first time my heart sat in deep realization that Raphael was in the middle of a different kind of story. We were out walking in the neighborhood park where his parents lived. We now lived a state away, and every visit back home was more telling that Dad's state of mind was ever-changing. He would wander off, and so would Grant. He would at times be more aggressive without knowing it, and so would Grant. He would suddenly shout at you, and so would Grant. Communicating acceptably was a significant challenge for both of them. Raphael excelled at communicating. He'd received multiple awards and acknowledgments for his excellence in the field of journalism, and the way in which he told stories. Now he stood in the middle of one. There was no book idea when I took this photo. No foreshadowing that this photo would one day be on the cover of the most difficult story that Raphael would be positioned to cover. All along, God had given this story to a gifted storyteller. I hug this moment still, while holding this book close to my heart. Papa, Raphael, and Grant on the cover, while grace covers all...

The Garage

Strange to say that I hate this photo. That's certainly not what I mean. What I hate though is that sometimes when I look at it, I hear everything that happened before this heart-breaking, albeit beautifully mending embrace. Grant wouldn't calm down. He was wrestling with a thought in his mind about what someone had said to him and the tone in which they said it to him. He had already punched a new hole into the wall, and the few holes that we were hopeful enough to have repaired, now needed repair again. Jesus.

The garage was that place where at least he could scream and swing it out, and the nearest neighbors knew, from many previous conversations, that we were trying. The disruptive sound of commotion was always the sound of us trying to get through the difficult moments. I heard a few half-empty paint cans fall and roll, but I heard Grant and Raphael rolling around too. The girls were in their rooms, the safest place for them. It broke me to realize that all of us were here together, yet in the moment we had to be apart.

I sat on the bottom stair, staring at the new hole in the wall. My husband, my best friend, my lover, those were his gut-wrenching cries. My only son, those were his ear-shattering screams. And now my inaudible cries and screams are spilling over into my hands that are tightly cupped around my mouth. Silence. Complete silence. I don't know how long it took for that sound to be heard, but I heard it and it was even louder than the noise. I stood up quickly because it startled me entirely. I reached for the garage doorknob and gripped it like the moment was now gripping me. I wondered, "What am I going to see when I open this door? What will the aftermath look like this time?"

Their shirts were torn, but they were more whole than I'd ever seen them be. "I'm sorry Dad." "I love you son." "Do you forgive me, dad?" "Do you forgive me, son?" "I love you, Dad." "I love you more son."

No, I don't hate this photo. I treasure it. I took this picture. But love perfectly framed it...

A Shining Example

It is true that sometimes we've no idea what it takes to walk in another person's shoes. But sometimes, we've no idea what it takes to shine their shoes. To polish their shoes. The strength it takes just to hold their shoes steadily in hand, while your heart is absolutely shaken by a stampede of memories. I remember just looking at Raphael. He wasn't saying anything audibly, but the determination in the delicately dedicated way he was buffing his father's shoes, said everything. These were the shoes of the man who exemplified how to be a man. The shoes of the man who set the high bar for what a husband and father should be and say and do. These were the shoes of the man who for years spoke wisdom in abundance. These were the shoes of the man who played the piano and preached people happy. These were also the shoes of a man who could no longer stand in them. I saw a tear fall. Pair after pair after pair, another tear. To my eye, those shoes had shined for a while now. Somehow though Raphael needed more time with his father's shoes. More time to think about the ground his father had covered in these shoes. More time to think about the places he'd gone and the people whose lives he'd touched in these shoes. More time. We both had wondered together, how much more time. Those shoes looked even brighter now, almost mirroring my father-in-law's spectacular smile. Raphael had done a masterful job. He'd remembered everything his father taught him about shining shoes. He'd remembered too what his father taught him about being a present, and loving, and attentive husband and father. That is the shine dad would be most proud of...

RSVP

Raphael never asks for anything for his birthday. Well, correction. There is a perfectly moist, incomparably delicious, red velvet cake baked by the mother of one of my dearest friend's that he absolutely loves. Even that request though has years placed between asks, as he never wants to "burden" anyone. But how many times do you turn fifty? Once, if you're honest. I persuaded him to have a birthday party with a gathering of those people closest to his heart. Hesitantly, albeit finally, he agreed. "Babe, do you think anyone will come?" I nodded my head yes. The invite list had the names of family, friends, co-workers, and neighbors. We smiled as the RSVP's steadily came in. There was one name, however, that caused me to take a deep breath every single time I looked at it. One person who I prayed between anxious breaths would really be there. One person who I really don't believe we could have possibly had this celebration without. Grant Raphael James. I'd written his name down by faith. "God please let our son be there." A couple of months before, Grant had to receive professional help outside of our home. For the first time, love alone wasn't enough to keep him here at home. Or maybe for the first time, love was strong enough to know he needed to go. Grant was better when he returned but there were still challenges. Still, days when we struggled to deal with the fact that this was truly our lives. The week of Raphael's birthday party arrived. I made sure the decorations and party favors were coming. I made sure that the cake with the large microphone made of buttercream icing was coming. I made sure that the people who promised they would be there were still coming. But my heart wanted desperately to know if Grant was coming. He did. Grant was right there smiling. He did so great during the party. He was his best and truest and friendliest self the entire time. The deep cry I'd been holding in for months found its way out during my remarks to Raphael. He held me, and God held us. James, party of five, present...

29

Acknowledgements

Thank you for journeying with us even if our travels just started with this book. Our family is keenly aware of the love and well-wishes extended to us by our villagers. We could not make it without our community, and I count you now as a part of our tribe. I want to thank my creator for literally, speaking to me during the penning of this memoir. I am grateful for the peace that comes with fulfilling this mission.

To my mother, LaDoris James, words cannot express how grateful I am to call you mother. I cherish and value your wisdom and dedication. Please forgive me for any pain I may have caused you.

To my siblings and extended family, there is no one like you. Thank you for your love and continued support. Thank you for hearing my heart.

To the healthcare workers who tended to my father during his illness, thank you. For the kindness that you extended to my mother and siblings, it did not go unnoticed. Thank you.

To every teacher, therapist, social worker, staff member, community friend, classmate, random stranger, checkout clerk, police officer, and Emergency Room staffer, who has ever taken the time to see my son and celebrate him for the kind prince that he is, I thank you. My family thanks you.

And to the one who is wondering how they will make it through this challenging time, to you I say hang in there. Don't be afraid or ashamed to talk to someone. A preacher, a teacher, a therapist, anyone you trust. Don't try to hold the pain inside. We all need to talk every now and then. If you can't talk it out, write it out, but by all means, get it out. And even if it doesn't seem that things are ever going to change, TRUST GOD ANYWAY.

About the Author: Raphael James

For more than two decades, Raphael James has been a trusted journalist and anchor for WCSC's Live Five News, bringing the day's most important stories into homes across the Lowcountry. With nearly 30 years in the field, he has covered historic moments—from exclusive interviews at the White House to the tragic Mother Emanuel AME Church massacre in Charleston, SC. A proud graduate of Paine College, Raphael's journalism career began in radio before transitioning to television, where he quickly rose through the ranks. Today, he and co-anchor Ann McGill have made history as the first Black main anchor team at WCSC-TV.

Beyond the newsroom, Raphael is deeply committed to his community, faith, and family. A member of Kappa Alpha Psi Fraternity, Inc., he has always woven service into his life's work. He is happily married to his college sweetheart, Sarena, and they share three wonderful children—Jaydn, Nia, and Grant. With *I Don't Want to Talk About It*, Raphael brings his storytelling beyond the screen, offering a powerful exploration of resilience, and courage to give voice to the truths we'd often rather leave unspoken.

I DON'T WANT TO TALK ABOUT IT